8.00
me

PARISH PRIESTS
AMONG THE SAINTS

ST. JOHN BAPTIST VIANNEY
Parish Priest of Ars

PARISH PRIESTS AMONG THE SAINTS

CANONIZED OR BEATIFIED PARISH PRIESTS

By

Father Walter Gumbley, O.P.

Foreword by

FATHER VINCENT McNABB, O.P., S.T.M.

Biography Index Reprint Series

BOOKS FOR LIBRARIES PRESS
FREEPORT, NEW YORK

First Published 1947

Revised edition first published 1955

Reprinted 1971 by arrangement with the
Trustees of Blackfriars, Oxford, England

INTERNATIONAL STANDARD BOOK NUMBER:
0-8369-8061-1

LIBRARY OF CONGRESS CATALOG CARD NUMBER:
76-148214

PRINTED IN THE UNITED STATES OF AMERICA

This Book is Dedicated
to the Saintly Memory of
MGR. HIPPOLYTE CONVERT
who for fifty years was
CURÉ D'ARS

Letter from the
RIGHT REVEREND JOHN McNULTY
Lord Bishop of Nottingham

BISHOP'S HOUSE,
THE PARK,
NOTTINGHAM.
March 12th, 1940.

My dear Father,

I gladly give my "imprimatur" to the enclosed which will be a delightful book and should do much good.

It will be a source of encouragement also to all those who are engaged in Apostolic work and who may sometimes be tempted to discouragement, feeling that "Mary" seems to be almost banished from their lives by "Martha".

Every kind wish and blessing,

Yours devotedly in Christ,

✠ JOHN, *Bishop of Nottingham.*

AUTHOR'S PROTESTATION

I SUBMIT this work to the infallible judgment of the Holy See; and in accordance with the decrees of Pope Urban VIII and other Roman Pontiffs, I protest that the report or account of any miracles and virtues, other than those already approved by the Holy See, rest on human authority alone; and also that in using the title of *Saint* or *Blessed* of any person neither canonized nor beatified there is no intention of anticipating or forestalling the decisions of the Holy See.

CONTENTS

Foreword by
Father Vincent McNabb, O.P., S.T.M.

THIS little book on canonized and beatified parish
priests has a value far beyond the number of its
pages. Its careful history of the parish priests,
secular and regular, thus honoured by the Church
is of great value in these days when salt that has
lost its savour will not need to wait long for those
who will cast it out and trample it under foot.

A common and most endearing quality of these
heroes of holiness is their fear; which, in spite of
their undeniable heroism, seemed almost a form of
cowardice. So greatly did they fear the account
they would have to render of their flock that sometimes the timid soul could not rid itself of a desire
for the desert.

Two motives lay behind their fears and desires.
Each of the two was so subtle as to deceive or
confuse even the elect.

The first of these motives urging the desert was
rooted in a clear recognition of the limitations of
parochial organization; which they scrupulously
attributed to the limitations of their own holiness and
zeal. It was hard for them, as it is still hard for us
to recognise that the Church is not merely or
primarily a Fold; it is also and primarily a Flock.

A Flock is ONE, but it is immovable. Moreover,
the encircling wall that makes a fold one is not for
unity and life, but for defence against the thief's and
the wolf's menace of death. Sheep penned always
within the fold die or die out.

9

How different is a flock, not encircled by a
defensive wall but led by the shepherd of the Flock.
Like a Fold a Flock is one; but unlike a Fold a
Flock is movable, with that self-movement which is
life.   Day by day the Flock lives and grows as it
moves under its shepherd from one pasture to
another.

Moreover its unity is not the imperfect and local
unity of a place made safe for sheep by a wall and
a gate.   The unity of a Flock is the perfect
psychological unity of a collective personality
moving towards its end under the guiding will of the
one "who has care of the sheep".

All this means that the parish unit, so necessary
for the defence of the flocks, is therefore defensive
and preservative rather than apostolic.   When that
function of defence is guaranteed by an endowment,
the parish tends to become a living; until in the
end "a good living" does not mean a parish with
good people, but a parish with a good income.

Men like the Curé d'Ars, who were all that
holiness could make a parish priest to be, were so
overwhelmed by the scanty harvest they reaped
that they laid the blame on themselves, the
harvesters.   In moments when the harvest seemed
light, and only the tares heavy, flight from the flock
into the desert seemed to be their only mercy to the
flock they had to feed.

*   *   *   *

The second motive behind their desire for the
desert was the longing to enjoy God in contemplation.   We know what their humility kept them

from knowing; that they were true shepherds of their flock and that their success was because their outer work of action welled up from an inner life of contemplation.

Now contemplation, being a foretaste of the bliss of heaven, tends to be an end in itself. Such joy and peace are given the soul in whom God shows Himself, that God must seem to drive them from His presence, like the Magdalen, that they may be perfect by doing His will.

The writer of this little book has gleaned so reverently and untiringly in the lives and amid the fears and desires of these souls, that what we are offered in its few pages are as gold, frankincense and myrrh.

FR. VINCENT MCNABB, O.P.

Introduction

IT has sometimes been stated that, with the single exception of Saint John Vianney, no parish priest has been declared a saint. Henri Ghéon, in his *Secret of the Curé d'Ars,* relates that the holy man was "terrified to learn that in the long roll of the ages not a single parish priest had been raised to the Church's altars as a saint. Popes had been canonized, cardinals, bishops, religious and laymen; but of parish priests not one; not the shadow of one."[1]

A constant and disturbing thought throughout the Curé's life was that he was living in a state of life in which it was uncommonly difficult to be a saint. His knowledge of hagiography was insufficient to show him that the short list of saints in any one particular calendar did not represent even two per cent of the total number of holy men and women whose claims to the title of Saint or Blessed have been ratified by the Church. So numerous, in fact, are the saints whose solemn veneration with both Office and Mass is permitted by the Holy See, that the *Johns* alone, if each were assigned his day in the calendar, would exceed the days of the year.

Moreover, even if the Curé did not know, his biographers should have known that in their own country, the eldest daughter of Christendom, is annually kept on May 19th the feast of the saintly parish priest of Louannec in Brittany, Saint Ivo, who died in 1303 in the very midst of his parochial duties, and was solemnly canonized by Pope Clement VI in 1347.

---

1 English Translation by F. J. Sheed, p. 123.

13

The study of Saint Ivo's life, first as a diocesan official, and then, for the last fifteen years of a short life of fifty, as a zealous pastor of souls, would have spared Saint John Vianney many months, even years, of troubled thought. He would have had no need to say to his curate, the faithful M. Toccanier: "I should be the happiest of priests, were it not for the thought that I must appear before the tribunal of God as a parish priest".[2] Neither would he have uttered the words repeated in a preliminary process of his beatification by Canon Camelet: "I should not like to die a parish priest, because I know of no saint who died in a like position".[3]

One other quotation may be cited from his own words to show how firmly fixed in his mind was this discouraging reflection. Speaking to a young subdeacon, he said: "This saint was a monk, that one a missionary; there are others of different callings. St. John Francis Regis and St. Vincent de Paul did not remain parish priests till the end of their days."[4]

Now amongst the great army of canonized and beatified saints, of whom not one fiftieth part can find space in any one particular calendar, there is an imposing group of saints who wrought their sanctification in feeding and tending the flock of Christ in the often obscure life of a parish priest. Of these many were martyrs, more were confessors; and whilst the greater number were members of the secular clergy, not a few were religious who won

---

2   Life by Trochu, Eng. Trans. by E. Graf, O.S.B., p. 550.
3   Ibid, p. 340.
4   Life by Monnin, French edit. 1867, vol. ii, p. 195.

their crowns in ministering to a particular parish. Moreover, great saints like Saint Dominic sometimes interrupted their ordinary ministry of preaching far and wide in order to take up for a period the duties and ties of parochial life. Finally we must remember that many holy parish priests who later became bishops or members of religious Orders, and as such have been canonized, had already attained to great sanctity in the performance of their pastoral duties.

The original parish priests of the Church were those who served the faithful in the days of persecution and many of them marched in the great army of martyrs. In the majority of cases even their names are lost, and of the remainder the details are very scanty. Many of them, too, faithful to the end, must be included in the army of glorious confessors who reign in heaven with the apostles, whose work in serving the flock of Christ they continued when on earth.

In this little book I aim only at presenting the reader with a sufficient answer to the question: "Have any parish priests been raised to the altars of the Church?", by giving short notes on the lives of three classes of priests, parish priests martyred, parish priests, already saints, who resigned their charge to enter upon a new state of life, and lastly those who died as confessors, acting as parish priests unto the end of their lives. I cannot claim to have made an exhaustive study of all the saints contained in the *Acta Sanctorum* of the Bollandists, a work running into seventy volumes, averaging a thousand pages a volume, each page in its turn averaging one-thousand words. But what I have gathered here will, I feel confident, go far to settle a question which need never have arisen; and also help to banish from the minds of a hard-working and devoted parochial clergy "the melancholy inference"—to quote once more from Henri Ghéon— "that there is no condition in the whole world in which sanctity is more difficult to attain".

One fact, however, will probably strike the imagination of the reader of this little book, the fact that the holiest saints dreaded the awful responsibility of souls, and, even amongst some of those whose lives are here recorded, there were a number, having the Curé d'Ars in their ranks, who tried to flee the burden but nevertheless endured the responsibility to the end. This book does not include all the priests of the secular clergy canonized or beatified. Far from it. Their number is great and their persons well known. Some of them, St. Vincent de Paul amongst their number, served parishes for a time, and some of them like St. John Kenty, patron saint of Galicia, ran away after being appointed parish priests.

Whilst this work was in the press the writer received the sad news of the death, on January 16, 1940, of the Right Reverend Mgr. Hippolyte Convert, Curé d'Ars since the year 1889. This saintly priest who in his life and work so closely resembled his canonized predecessor, had already expressed his pleasure on reading portions of this book, which appeared in abbreviated form in the *Rosary Magazine* of 1939. It was hoped to dedicate the completed work to him; it is now dedicated to his saintly memory.

CHAPTER I

The Early Centuries

1. ST. NEPOTIAN,

Priest of Altino near Venice. Died 395.

AMONGST the writings of St. Jerome is a letter
of sympathy written to Bishop Heliodorus of
Altino in 395 on the death of his nephew Nepotian
a saintly young priest who had worked zealously for
souls in that small episcopal city, since destroyed,
which lay near the ancient patriarchal see of Aquileia
afterwards transferred to Venice. Nepotian had
been an officer in the imperial bodyguard but gave
up his splendid prospects and sold all his goods for
the benefit of the poor in order to serve God solely.
His fear of the responsibilities of the priesthood held
him back from ordination for a considerable time but
eventually he allowed himself to be persuaded by
his uncle and was by him ordained and given a
ministerial charge in Altino where he laboured with
remarkable zeal until his early death.

Fr. Thurston says it is difficult to trace a cult to
him but cites the Bollandists who give a notice of
him on May 11. Thurston himself and Mgr. Holweck
give May 4 as the day of his feast.

Acta Sanctorum, May 11; Fr. Herbert Thurston's ed. of
Butler's Lives of the Saint, May 4; Mgr. F. G. Holweck,
Biographical Dictionary of the Saints, Herder, 1924, p. 732;
Migne, P.L. xxii, pp. 527-40, 589-602.

2. ST. FORTUNATUS,

Parish Priest of Torrita.   Fifth century.

IN the Roman Martyrology, under June 1, we
read: "In Umbria, the feast of Saint Fortunatus
the priest, glorious for his virtues and miracles".

Fortunatus lived about the year 400, and was the
priest in charge of the parish of Torrita in the
diocese, and not far from the city of Spoleto. Like
many of the early parish priests he worked with his
hands, and his profession was farming which he
seems to have followed in order to get more money
for the poor. Ploughing one day he turned up two
pennies which without more ado he slipped into his
pocket and went on with his work, until interrupted
by a shout from the edge of the field. It was a
beggar calling out for an alms, and Fortunatus bade
him go over to the presbytery, adding that he
himself would be along in a few minutes. With the
importunity of his class the tramp refused to wait
and demanded immediate relief. He seemed to see
in the saint's suggestion an intention of putting him
off. But Fortunatus, far from being offended,
unbuttoned his tunic and gave him his small
treasure-trove. As he did so he noticed the coins
were gold pieces, not pennies, but all the same
willingly parted with them. We are not expressly
told by his biographer, Audelaus the priest, that
there had been a miraculous change, but
undoubtedly we are supposed to infer that from the
narrative.

In fact Fortunatus was wholly devoted to the care
of the poor, the sick and the suffering, and Audelaus

says that his love of charity was sharpened by his love of poverty. As befitted a husbandman he was buried in his own field, where soon a splendid church was erected in his memory by a wealthy man, delivered by his intercession from an unjust imprisonment. Many other miracles were worked at his tomb, including the cure of three lepers, and two blind men. A legend is preserved to the effect that a stick, with which he urged on his team of oxen, when planted in the earth grew into a tree whose leaves provided an antidote for poison.

The feast of St. Fortunatus is kept on June 1, and he is the patron of the city of Montefalco, near Torrita.

Acta SS. of the Bollandists, t. 21 (June 1), pp. 72-4; Holweck, *Biographical Dictionary of the Saints* (Herder) 1924, p. 394.

3. ST. OSTIAN,

Parish Priest of Viviers. Fifth century.

NO details have been preserved to us of this saint whose commemoration in the Roman Martyrology occurs on June 30. His cult however dates back to the earliest times, and his feast is annually celebrated at Viviers and Le Puy, at the former place as a greater double, at the latter as a semi-double. Holweck suggests that he preached the gospel in Velay, but there seems no reason to doubt that he was the regional priest of Viviers some time in the fifth century.

Acta SS., t. 27 (June 30), pp. 540-1; Holweck, p. 761.

4. ST. AMABILIS,

Parish Priest of Riom.   Died 475.

THIS early French parish priest is said to have
    died on November 1, 475.   Details of his life
are practically non-existent beyond the statement
that he was noted for the spiritual and temporal care
of his flock, and, that having a great devotion to
Saint John the Baptist and Saint Benignus the
martyr, he erected a church to the honour of each.
By his preaching he converted many.   He died at an
advanced age and was buried in the Church of Saint
Benignus.

He is a member of that large group of saints, who,
like St. Paul, St. Hilary and St. Patrick, rid the
surrounding countryside of venomous snakes.
There are, however, critics who state that the thirty
or more saints to whom this benefaction is attributed, did it allegorically, by casting out the far
more poisonous serpents of false doctrines.   Be that
as it may, and granting that St. Amabilis rid the
Auvergne district of the serpents of paganism, it is
no mere legend that his help has constantly been
sought and found by those bitten by adders.   Two
such cases of his heavenly assistance, both well
attested and both occurring in the year 1650, may
be cited here.

A surgeon, who was extracting poison from an
adder to serve as an anti-toxin, was so badly bitten
on the hand as to be given up for lost, and a priest
was hurriedly summoned to give him the last
sacraments.   Then the dying man was carried to the
saint's tomb in Riom where the wound was

touched with a relic, one of the saint's teeth.
Immediately poisonous matter began to escape from
the bitten hand, and in a short time the surgeon
recovered.

The second case was no less striking.   A
Franciscan, walking, according to the rules of his
Order, with sandals only protecting his bare feet,
was unfortunate enough to tread on an adder which
fastened its fangs in his foot.   Groaning with pain
he was carried on horseback to the same church,
that of St. Benignus, and he too was immediately
restored to health.

These two miracles were witnessed by a great
number of both clergy and laity, as also were the
contemporary cures of a little girl of eight and a
young man of twenty-five.   To the bystanders it
was a truly awe-inspiring sight to behold the power
of God thus manifested through the intercession of
a saint who lived nearly twelve hundred years
before.

The feast of St. Amabilis is kept as a double
throughout the diocese of Clermont on October 18,
and that of the translation of his relics, on June 11.

Acta SS., t. 22 (June 11), pp. 460-5; Holweck, p. 55.

5. ST. SEVERUS,

Parish Priest of Saxia in Bigorre.   Fifth century.

WE have no certain date of this parish priest and
saint beyond the fact that St. Gregory of Tours,
who wrote his life, himself died in 594.

What St. Gregory tells us, though scanty, is of interest in showing that these early parish priests like many of their successors today, had to serve more than one church, and had sometimes to cover a considerable distance in this double ministry. One Sunday, being rather late and leaving Saxia in a hurry, Severus spurred his horse over sharply so that the animal ran too close to a tree at the side of the road, causing the saint to smack his head soundly against an overhanging bough. If we can say such a thing of so holy a man we should be tempted to admit that Severus sadly lost his temper, for dismounting from his horse he cursed the tree, in the name of God, root and branch, and so continued on his way.

He was accustomed to remain at his second church until the Wednesday of the following week; and this time on his return journey he noticed that the offending tree had died, and that nothing remained but the stricken bole and the withered branches. Sunday's painful incident was thus brought back to his mind together with the recollection of his fit of temper. Severely blaming himself for his fault he now called on God to restore life to the tree, which straightway revived sending forth new shoots.

The feast of St. Severus is celebrated in the diocese of Tarbes and Lourdes on September 7, with the rank of a double.

Patrologia Latina, Migne, t. 71, nos. 934, 935; Holweck, p. 907; Dictionary of Christian Biography, Smith and Wace, iv, p. 641; Acta SS., t. 35 (Aug. 1), pp. 55-6.

6. ST. SEVERUS,

Parish Priest of Interocrea.   Died 530.

THIS saint is commemorated by St. Gregory the
Great in his Dialogues and finds a place in the
Roman Martyrology under the date, February 15.
He was parish priest of Interocrea in the Abruzzi
and his death is recorded to have taken place in the
year 530.   St. Gregory relates that one day when
he was busy dressing his vines—for like other early
parish priests he worked in the fields or vineyards—
Severus was hastily called to the house of a notorious
sinner who was thought to be at the last extremity.
The saint promised to be along in a moment, but
stayed to finish some small task.   When he got to
the house the neighbours ran out to meet him with
the news that the man was dead, "Holy Father,
why did you delay?   But be not disturbed now,
for behold the man is already dead."

The saint however was very much disturbed, as
any parish priest would be in similar circumstances,
and rushing into the house, flung himself on the floor
at the side of the body and calling himself a murderer
of the dead man's soul, wept for his negligence with
so bitter a sorrow that God to comfort his servant
raised the dead man to life.   Thereupon, with much
contrition and devotion the resuscitated man received
from the saint the last sacraments, and after seven
days spent in lamenting his former sins sank back
quietly into death on the eighth day.

With the single exception of this act of careless-
ness, Severus lived as a model pastor, and the father

of the poor and sick. On the former he spent most
of his earnings, and of the latter it was told how,
when too ill to go to the saint themselves, they
begged their friends to bring back some of the bread
the holy man was accustomed to bless, and by its
means they regained health.

St. Severus was buried at Orvieto, but in the
tenth century his remains were granted as a most
blessed gift to the abbey of Meinfeldt in the diocese
of Trier, where his feast is still kept, on February
15. The dioceses of Rieti and Aquila also annually
commemorate him.

Patrol. Lat., Migne, t. 77, pp. 212-3; Acta SS., t. 5
(Feb. 15), pp. 826-9; Holweck, p. 907.

7. ST. FREDERIC,

Priest of Vlierzeele in East Flanders.
Early seventh century.

ST. FREDERIC (or Flederic) was born of Christian
parents dwelling near Paris who brought him
up so well that, as his biographer tells us, "the
religion he professed at baptism he fostered throughout his youth", and after earnest study he was
admitted to the priesthood and given charge of the
church in Vlierzeele in East Flanders "where he
instilled true doctrine and piety into his flock". He
has always been ranked amongst the patron saints
of the deaf owing to his miracle in silencing the voices
of numerous and noisy toads which disturbed his
services both in the early and late hours of the day,
a miracle not uncommon in hagiography.

All this is recounted by Cornelius van Gestel in his history of the see of Malines, vol. ii, 305. The Bollandists who quote van Gestel at length, add that Frederic's name appears in several ancient martyrologies, but state that there is no clue to the century in which he lived.   We know however that his pastorate was before Saint Bavo built a monastery there, and that Bavo died in 653.

In 1545 Bishop Martin Cupper, auxiliary to Cambrai, fixed the feast of St. Frederic on September 13.

Acta SS., Sept., t. iv, pp. 133 seq.; Holweck, pp. 387, 403.

8. ST. WERENFRID,

Parish Priest of Elst.   Died 760.

ON August 14 is annually celebrated in the metropolitan Cathedral of Utrecht the feast of St. Werenfrid, an English priest who accompanied St. Willibrord to Holland to evangelize the then pagan people dwelling there.   Werenfrid settled down at Elst where he established a flourishing mission and built a church.   He then removed to Westervoost where he also set up a parish and church.   He was buried at Elst, and his tomb was the scene of many miracles.   The Bollandists resist the claim of the Benedictines that he belonged to their Order, and maintain that he was a secular priest.

Acta SS., t. 40 (Aug. 27), pp. 100-5; Holweck, pp. 1032, 1033; Stanton's *Menology of England and Wales,* London 1887, pp. 393-4.

c

9. BLESSED GAMELBERT,
Parish Priest of Michaelsbuch. Died about 790.

A LMOST eleven centuries before the days of the
Curé d'Ars, there dwelt in Germany a parish
priest whose life was in a great number of ways a
striking parallel to his.   Like St. John Vianney
the Blessed Gamelbert stoutly resisted the military
calling, ardently sought the service of God, and
being of mediocre talents had this deficiency supplied by grace as a reward for his purity of heart and
consuming zeal.   Similarly he lived a life of
astonishing hardship, was a lover of the poor, a
peacemaker, and above all unwearied in the
confessional.

He came of a soldier's family and his father
mapped out for him a glorious career of arms. He
used to tie a belt and sword round the boy's waist,
but, we are told, they always fell off—probably a
pious expression of the saint's biographer to explain
the boy letting them fall.

Eventually his father capitulated and Gamelbert
became the priest of his own native town. On his
father's death he succeeded to the estate, which he
employed for the benefit of the poor. He refused to
dwell in the family mansion and contented himself
with a roughly built cabin he set up against the walls
of the church. Here during the whole of Lent he
used to enclose himself completely, said Mass in the
church behind a thick curtain and would not even
give Holy Communion to his flock, leaving this duty
to his deacon. But he continually heard confessions
from the little window of his cabin.

His love of purity was angelic, and was rendered
so by a signal victory over an evil woman in his
youth.   First of all he expostulated with her, tried
to bring her mind back from sin to God, but as she
continued in her evil solicitation, he took to his heels
and ran from the place with all his might.

His patience under calumnies, his winning smile
and gentleness cannot but bring to mind him of
Ars.   He was ever a great peacemaker and we read
of his intervening in disputes and even violent
street fights; and he was invariably successful in
persuading the combatants to desist.   His way with
quarrelsome domestics would not commend itself to
all masters.   When trouble broke out he used first
to attempt peace by words, but these failing he
would distribute money, goods or even some of his
garments among them.   The fact that he possessed
servants, whilst he lived by himself in a tiny wooden
house, may seem at first sight incongruous, but his
biographer almost certainly means us to understand
by the word servants, those whom the saint retained
to look after the family mansion, which was still in
his possession, and very probably also those bound
to the soil and dwelling on the family lands.   The
laws of the day would not permit of an emancipation
of these *en masse,* although we read that the saint
gave freedom to many.   The ancestral home seems
to have been the residence which Gamelbert's
successor, Blessed Utto, turned into a monastery.

In sacred art Gamelbert is depicted baptising an
infant, the infant being Blessed Utto, whose parents
persuaded Gamelbert to baptize him when he passed
through their country on his pilgrimage to Rome.

Whether Utto was born in Italy or Switzerland or Germany, we are left in doubt. Equally doubtful is the time of Gamelbert's journey, but it must have been considerably earlier than the golden jubilee of his priesthood as suggested in his oldest biography, to allow Utto time to grow up and be ordained priest as his successor in the parish.

When Gamelbert was a very old man his parishioners besought him to name a successor from amongst the many excellent priests in the surrounding country, but the saint bade them wait a year and God would sent his chosen one. When the appointed twelve months had elapsed Blessed Utto arrived, and to him Gamelbert handed over everything in connection with his office, whilst he himself prepared for death which overtook him on January 27, somewhere about the year 790.

We have mentioned similarities between Blessed Gamelbert and St. John Vianney, and to complete them we may notice the great storm that occurred at the death of each. The one that synchronized with Gamelbert's death was a fearful affair, and so great were the torrents of rain that fell that the people were afraid to go to his funeral. But the bolder ones carried the body to the church, and on the following day although the tempest still raged they proceeded with the obsequies. No sooner had they begun than the rain and wind ceased, only however to recur with renewed violence as soon as the body was committed to the grave. The sacred relics were later placed under the high altar of the church, which became the scene of many miracles, particularly the healing of those crippled.

In 1909 Saint Pius X confirmed the immemorial cult paid to Gamelbert and his disciple Utto.   The feast of the former is a double in the diocese of Ratisbon.   The latter saint early retired into monastic life and consequently does not find a place in this book.

Acta SS., t. 3 (Jan. 27), pp. 398-400; Holweck, p. 413; Matthew Rader, S.J., *Bavaria Sancta* (1617); Acta Apost. Sedis, vol. i, pp. 752-5.

10. ST. WAMBERT,

Parish Priest of St. Pierre-sur-Dive in Normandy. Martyred in the ninth century.

THE only details that have come down to us of the life of Saint Wambert (Vambert or Vandobert) are that he was in charge of the church of St. Pierre-sur-Dive in Normandy in the ninth century and was cruelly put to death for his faith by the Norman invaders.   His body was one of the most sacred treasures of the abbey of Dive before the French Revolution, and his feast was annually celebrated on June 26.

Acta SS., June, t. 7, pp. 200, 201; Holweck, p. 1006.

11. ST. FLORINUS,

Parish Priest of Remus in Switzerland.   Died about 856.

THERE is a tradition that St. Florinus was the son of a Briton and a converted Jewess, a couple who after making a pilgrimage to Rome settled at Matsch in the Vintschgau, where their son was born. His education was entrusted to Alexander, parish priest of Remus, who had him ordained and appointed his own curate.

On his benefactor's death St. Florinus took over the charge of the parish and died there on November 17, about the year 856. Many miracles were attributed to him both in his lifetime and after his death, including the changing of water into wine; and his tomb at Remus is still a place of pilgrimage. During the Middle Ages his body was transferred to the cathedral church at Chur in which diocese Remus lies, but in the year 1501 it was brought back to its first resting place at Remus. His feast is kept on the day of his death, being a double of the first class with an octave at Chur, of which city and cathedral he is patron.

Holweck, p. 391.

CHAPTER II

The Middle Ages

12. ST. GRIMOALD,

Parish Priest of Pontecorvo. Lived about 1130.

ABOUT the year 1130 we find mention of St.
Grimoald, parish priest and rural dean of
Pontecorvo near Aquino, whose commemoration in
the Roman Martyrology occurs under the date
September 29. The legend runs that he and his two
brothers, SS. Fulk and Eleutherius, made a pilgrimage to Rome from their home in England. Fulk
remained a pilgrim and died helping the plague-
stricken in the diocese of Aquino. Eleutherius
passed his days as a hermit in the kingdom of
Naples, whilst the remaining brother, Grimoald,
dwelt as a parish priest at Pontecorvo just outside
the Neapolitan border, where in commemoration of
St. John the Baptist he built a splendid church.

In 1725 Pope Benedict XIII added the title of
Pontecorvo to that of the bishop of Aquino, raising
Grimoald's church to the rank of a cathedral with
its own chapter of canons. Here Grimoald's
feast is kept as a greater double for he ranks
as a patron of the city. According to his
biographer, an early bishop of Aquino, St. Grimoald
was famous both in life and death for many
miracles.

Acta. SS., t. 48 (September 29), pp. 184-5; Holweck,
p. 453; Stanton's *Menology,* p. 240.

13. ST. WILLIAM,

Parish Priest of Pontoise.   Died 1193.

A^N Englishman by birth and descent, William settled in France sometime in the middle of the twelfth century, and was given charge of a parish in Pontoise where the king of France, Philip Augustus, had a palace and it was in this building that the saint expired after he had been carried in a dying condition from the ranks of the Rogation procession he was attending on May 10, 1193. He was very highly thought of by King Philip, who gave him his last shelter on earth, and was also present at his death. St. William's reputation as a saint sprang up immediately at his death, and at Pontoise his feast is kept on May 10 as a double; while at Versailles it is kept on the following day.

Acta SS., t. 14 (May 3); Holweck, p. 1036; Stanton's *Menology*, p. 206.

14. ST. WALHERE,

Parish Priest of Onhaye in Belgium.   Died 1209.

S_{AINT} WALHERE, a native of Bouvignes near Dinant, was parish priest of Onhaye near Namur, and archpriest or rural dean of Florennes. In this position he was no respecter of persons, correcting abuses wherever he found them. In the course of his duty he had the painful task of severely reprimanding the loose living parish priest at

Hastière, who was his own nephew. This man appeared to take in good part the corrections and warnings of his uncle the dean, and graciously enough offered to row him back up the Meuse to his house at Onhaye. It was early morning and intensely dark, but St. Walhere evidently wished to say Mass in his own church. Taking advantage of the darkness the unnatural nephew rose up and crushed his uncle's head with an oar, and threw the body into the river. We are left in ignorance of the fate that overtook the murderer, but the holy body was discovered floating on the surface of the water, and was interred with great honour by his parishioners in the church of St. Martin which Walhere had erected.

There the remains have rested enshrined, a centre for many pilgrimages; and miracles took place at his tomb up to the time that the Bollandists collected their materials for his biography. In the year 1634 Pope Urban VIII extended the many privileges already conferred on the Confraternity of St. Walhere by granting a plenary indulgence to those who communicated on his feast, which in the cathedral city and diocese of Namur is kept on June 27.

Acta SS., t. 25 (June 23), pp. 523-32; Holweck, p. 1031.

15. BLESSED GONSALVO OF AMARANTE, O.P.

Sometime Parish Priest of Riva de Vizella in Portugal.   Died 1259.

BLESSED GONSALVO, Gundisalvus or Gonzalez, was born about the year 1187 at Vizella in the diocese of Braga, Portugal's metropolitan see, and was a member of a rich family. He was educated for the priesthood in the archbishop's own household, and was given the extremely comfortable living of St. Pelagia, a parish in Riva de Vizella.

Gonsalvo spent almost the whole of his time and fortune on his parishioners. He regarded his considerable revenues as a trust he held for those in want, and his large presbytery became a lodging-house for the sick and for pilgrims. Early writers of saints' lives almost unanimously employ the word *peregrini* instead of *vagabundi,* but there is little doubt that these same pilgrims would be those described by us today as tramps.

Blessed Gonsalvo's chief devotion was to the Sacred Passion, and he longed to visit the Holy Places. At length he sought and obtained permission from his archbishop to visit both Palestine and Rome, having assured both himself and that prelate that he had an excellent substitute as administrator of his parish in the person of his nephew, a very pious priest.

Gonsalvo's pilgrimage proved a lengthy one, but Father Diego of the Rosary, his biographer, rather strains our credulity in asking us to believe it

extended over fourteen years.   "Voluntarily," he
adds, "would the saint have finished his days in the
Holy Land, but his pastoral solicitude bade him
return to Portugal, once more to take up the care of
the souls entrusted to him."   Father Diego can
scarcely expect us to believe that the pastoral
solicitude of so holy a priest would not have urged
him to a more speedy return.

Leaving this problem in hagiography, and return-
ing with the saint to Vizella, we find the nephew a
very changed man from the good young priest his
uncle had left in charge.   "Gone to the dogs" was
literally a true expression in this case, for he had
"filled his kennels with valuable dogs and the
stables with beautiful horses," whilst the presbytery, in his uncle's day the resort, as we have said,
of the poor and sick, was now full of his hunting
companions.   He had also spread about a rumour
of his uncle's death; but in this, in view of the
"fourteen years", he could scarcely be blamed. He
had, however, without consulting anyone taken
formal possession of the benefice as canonical parish
priest.

When the saint arrived home the nephew refused
to recognize him, and it is more than possible that
he did not believe him genuine, seeing the condition
of dire poverty in which Gonsalvo presented himself.
But this did not excuse him for setting his dogs upon
the saint, and it was only with difficulty that Gonsalvo was rescued from their fangs by the servants.
Covered with wounds he withdrew, leaving his
nephew in his ill-gotten charge unmolested, without
appealing to the archbishop for justice.   He took it

as a sign that God had released him from a burden which he had always felt too heavy for him; and went into a less known part of the countryside to spend the remainder of his life in prayer and solitude. This was the same desire of solitude that in future centuries was to prove such a temptation to the Curé d'Ars. But Gonsalvo would not give up entirely his pastoral duties. He began to evangelize the badly instructed peasants of the district and other neglected souls, and built a small chapel at a place called Amarante which locality has given him the surname by which he has ever since been called. This oratory, dedicated to the Holy Mother of God, became the centre of religion for many.

But he was still undecided about his future, and we are told he prayed incessantly for some manifestation of the Divine Will. At length, Our Blessed Lady in a vision directed him to enter amongst the friars newly devoted to God and her especial honour, who had recently settled in Portugal. Gonsalvo thereupon applied for admission to the Dominican prior of Guimaraens, himself since beatified as Blessed Peter Gonzalez. Gonsalvo was at once accepted and after his year of novitiate was completed and he had taken his vows, he obtained leave to return to his work of evangelization at Amarante which he continued until his death; so that in fact he remained in the charge of souls to the end of his life, and for this reason should be given an honourable place in the ranks of canonized and beatified parish priests.

One of the works he set himself to do, on his return, was the construction of a bridge over the river Tamarga which flowed by his little church, and many wonders are told of him during this period of his life.   One day he struck a rock from which gushed wine to quench the thirst of his voluntary helpers.   Another day there came a miraculous catch of fish when they were hungry.

These miracles Blessed Gonsalvo shares with other saints, and indicate how all through the early ages bridge-building was truly accepted as one of the great works of mercy.   Similar wonders, for example, are told of his former prior, Blessed Peter Gonzalez already mentioned.   Gonsalvo's interest in his bridge did not cease with his death, for when in the year 1400 a fearful inundation swept over the countryside, he was seen turning aside some oak trees which were being dashed against it.

From the day of his death he was venerated as a saint and all Portugal rejoiced when in 1565 the great Archbishop of Braga, Bartholomew of the Martyrs, prevailed upon the Pope, Pius IV, to ratify his cult and extend the privilege of a special Mass and Office in his honour, not only to the Dominican Order, but to the whole of the country.   His feast is kept on January 10.

Acta SS., t. 1 (Jan. 10), pp. 640-50; Holweck, p. 457, 458; Année Dominicaine, Lyons, t. 1, pp. 335-46; Touron, *Hommes Illustres de l'ordre de St. Dominique*, Paris, 1743, t. 1, pp. 61-75.

16. BLESSED THOMAS HELYE,

Parish Priest of St. Maurice, in the diocese of Coutances. Died 1257.

BLESSED THOMAS HELYE was another saintly parish priest in France who anticipated the holy life of the parish priest of Ars.   He was born at Biville in the diocese of Coutances in 1187, and studied in Paris where he chose as his confessor the celebrated scripture scholar, Hugh de St. Cher, author of the first concordance of the bible, and a man of eminent sanctity.   Hugh was also his professor in theology.

Thomas was late in entering the priesthood and his ordination did not take place much before his forty-fourth year.   He was one of the group of saintly persons with which St. Louis IX of France surrounded himself, and Thomas acted for some time as his almoner.   After a few years at court he returned to his native diocese and was given the administration of the parish of St. Maurice.   On his departure St. Louis gave him a set of silk vestments and a chalice of silver-gilt, gifts which were reverently preserved for many centuries.   Thomas ruled his parish but a short time, resigning it for a commission to preach missions throughout Normandy, and by the time of his death he had preached in each church several times.   His death took place at Vauville, Manche, October 19, 1257.

His daily life was one of the severest mortification. Every Friday he fasted on bread and water and during Lent he added Mondays, Wednesdays and

Saturdays to this list. Other days he lived very
poorly on a few vegetables and fish boiled without
salt. The fact that he dispensed himself from a bread
and water diet for three week-days in Lent was due
to the heavy labour entailed by his missionary
duties. His sleep too was wonderfully curtailed, so
that, as in the case of St. John Vianney, there did
not seem either sufficient food or rest to support a
human frame, yet both saints laboured assiduously
until they had reached seventy years. And like the
Curé d'Ars Blessed Thomas Helye spent the greater
part of his working day in the confessional.

Blessed Thomas, like another great preacher of
the Gospel, St. Dominic, used the church for what
scanty sleep he took. He seems never to have gone
to bed.   Both saints prayed long hours, almost
through the entire night, laying their tired frames on
the altar steps. And like St. Dominic he dreadfully
beat himself with heavy scourges. Amongst Blessed
Thomas's night prayers were daily included the
entire office of the Dead, the penitential and the
gradual psalms and the litanies of the Saints.

We are fortunate in having all this first hand
information   supplied   by   his   contemporary
biographer, a priest named Clement, who had access
to the process of canonization which was opened in
1261 but not completed and finally not persevered
with.   The reasons why the cause was not continued
were several, including the death of Cardinal de
saint Cher, his former professor and confessor, who
had been sent by Pope Clement IV to supervise the
proceedings which till then had been in the hands of
the bishop and the Dominican prior of Coutances.

It was their signed documents which Clement used. These two prelates give the sworn witness of many outstanding miracles wrought within a year of the saint's death. These included the raising to life of a little boy drowned in a well, and a girl of two and half years drowned in a pool.

These miracles continued through the centuries and the Bollandists record many that happened in the seventeenth century. Pius IX set the seal on his immemorial cult in 1857, the sixth centenary of the saint's death, by granting permission for Mass and Office to be said in his honour throughout the diocese of Coutances. His feast is kept on October 17.

Acta SS., t. 56 (Oct. 29), pp. 592-622; Holweck, p. 980.

17. BLESSED DAVANAZATO,

Parish Priest of Casciano near Florence. Died 1295.

THIS saint deserves to be far better known because, although details of him are scanty, there are more than sufficient to make him a most desirable patron of all who have the charge of souls. Born, it is said, about the year 1200 he became a parish priest in his twenty-fifth year and continued in this work until his death in 1295, having ruled the parish of St. Lucy in Casciano, in the valley of Elsa in the diocese of Florence, for seventy years.

As a parish priest his life resembled those of whom we have already spoken. The income of the parish was held by him as the property of the poor, and to

increase this income he lived himself on the scantiest
fare, and many times, in order that the poor should
not go hungry, he reduced his own meals to bread
and water.   Frequently his bed was lent to others
and he slept on the bare floor.   On more than one
occasion provisions were miraculously multiplied,
and once when he had invited the neighbouring
clergy to dinner on the feast of St. Lucy and found
there was no wine, he followed Our Lord's example
and bade his servant fill up a pot of water and pour
it into the empty tumblers, whereupon it became
most delicious wine.

Blessed Davanazato realised in his own person the
solemn words of Our Divine Lord in His prayer over
the Apostles: *For them do I sanctify myself, that
they also may be sanctified in truth.* (St. John xvii,
19.)   He knew there would be no sanctifying of his
parish unless he himself were sanctified personally
by mortification, fasting and prayer.   His prayer
was continuous and he always, like the Curé d'Ars
and so many other holy pastors, recited his Office
on his knees before the altar.

He was laid to rest in his own church of St. Lucy,
but in 1787 his relics were removed to the neighbouring parish church of St. Bartholomew in
Barberino where his feast is celebrated on July 7,
being usually preceded by a solemn triduum in his
honour.   Blessed Davanazato is venerated by the
Franciscans as a member of their Third Order.

Acta SS., t. 29 (July 7), pp. 524-9; Holweck, p. 264;
Lives of Franciscan Saints by Fr. Leo, trans. into English 1885,
vol. ii, pp. 441-5.

18.   BLESSED BARTOLO OF BUONPEDONI,
Parish Priest of Peccioli and Pichena.   Died 1300.

A PARISH priest and saint, contemporary with
Blessed Davanazato, and like him a Franciscan
Tertiary, was Blessed Bartolo (Bartholomew)
Buonpedoni, for many years pastor of Peccioli in
the diocese of Volterra.   He was born about the
year 1228 at Mucchio near San Gemignano of
parents possessing both rank and wealth.   This
combination of good fortune led his father and
mother to the usual desire of seeing their son make
a good match, but Bartolo, to escape a vocation to
which he felt he was not called, declined the
marriage state and entered the Benedictine abbey of
San Vito in Pisa.   But he was soon equally sure that
his vocation was no more to the religious life than it
was to matrimony.   It is said that his true call,
which was to the secular priesthood, was manifested
to him by Our Lord in a vision, in which He told the
saint that he would glorify Him by his sufferings as
a parish priest.

The saint then offered himself to the Bishop of
Volterra and at the age of thirty was ordained priest
and assigned to a cure of souls first at Peccioli, and
then at Pichena, where he worked as a model pastor
for twenty-two years.   The unwearying servant and
almoner of the poor, he showed particular charity to
any Franciscan or one connected with that Order of
which he himself had been a tertiary from the days
preceding his ordination.

In the year 1280, when he had reached his fifty-second year, the sufferings foretold to him in the vision came upon him in the form of a severe leprosy which remained incurable to the day of his death twenty years later, and forced him to resign his parish and go to dwell in a leper hospital at Celloli, of which he became at the same time patient, governor and chaplain, reminding us of that other great priest, Damien the Leper. Bartolo's disciple named Vivaldo, who acted as his general factotum in the parish, and his housekeeper Stella, with quiet but amazing heroism, refused to be parted from his service and accompanied him to Celloli to see that he was properly attended to. Of Stella it is related that she remained with her master until his death (December 12, 1300), and, as she knelt weeping by the side of his dead body, the corpse consoled her for her charity by reaching out and grasping her hand, holding it for a considerable time. Stella must have possessed uncommonly strong nerves.

Vivaldo, who also remained with the saint until the end, departed after his death to an hermitage he constructed near San Gemignano, and which consisted of a cell made out of the hollow trunk of a chestnut tree. Here he died in the odour of sanctity in 1302, two years after the death of Blessed Bartolo, and was raised to the altars by Saint Pius X as Blessed Vivaldo in 1909. Bartolo himself was beatified in the following year, April 19, 1910. His feast is kept on December 13, but the Franciscans celebrate it on the following day.

Acta Apostolicae Sedis, 1910, pp. 411-4; Holweck, p. 137; *Lives of Franciscan Saints,* vol. iv, pp. 165-9; Thurston's Butler, Dec. 12.

19. ST. IVO HELORY,

Parish Priest of Louannec in Brittany. Died 1303.

IT is due to careless history that Saint Ivo has come
to be regarded merely as a lawyer, because he
was the diocesan official of the Bishops of Rennes
and of Tréguier; and not only has the fact that he
died a parish priest been oftentimes forgotten, but
even the fact of his having been a priest at all. The
plain fact is that out of a not very long life of fifty
years he spent the last fifteen as a parish priest, and
died in the midst of his parochial duties; and his
solemn canonization forty-four years after his death
was the solemn canonization of a parish priest. How
this glory of the secular priesthood has come to be
overlooked even in France is one of those mysteries
of ignorance amongst popular writers that are only
too common, but not easily explained.

Saint Ivo was born in the castle of Kermartin in
Brittany in 1253, and being a more than ordinarily
gifted youth studied successfully arts, philosophy
and divinity at Paris, and rounded this off with a
brilliant course in civil and canon law at Orleans.
But Ivo had not yet made up his mind to enter the
ecclesiastical state, although he had already decided
he had no vocation to the married life, and had
early in his youth made a vow of chastity. Apart
from the brilliance of his mental gifts which made
him one of the most learned men in Brittany, he
closely resembled St. John Vianney in his life of
mortification.   Even as a youth St. Ivo gave up
sleeping in a bed, contenting himself with a rough

mat stretched on the ground, with a stone or a book, often his bible, as a pillow.

Though he refused marriage he was afraid to aspire to the priesthood, contenting himself with the clerical dignity conferred by tonsure and minor Orders. He served in the diocese of Rennes as ecclesiastical judge and the bishop of that see persuaded him to receive the subdiaconate and later the diaconate. His own diocesan, Bishop de Brieuc of Tréguier, now recalled him to his diocese and gave him the same judicial work to do.   He likewise placed him under obedience to receive the priesthood. Ivo had a tremendous fear of his new responsibilities as a priest, and the prospect of standing at the altar made him tremble, as do the Seraphim before the throne of God.   Those familiar with the life of the Curé d'Ars will remember how often he said it would be necessary to have the holiness of a Seraph to celebrate the Divine Mysteries.   "Pour dire La Messe il faudrait être un seraphin."

In his judicial duties St. Ivo looked always in fear to the Judge of all, Whom he strove to serve and please in all his actions. It is recorded that he often waived his dignity as a judge in order to plead as a simple advocate the cause of the poor in the lay courts, doing this without charge.   Little wonder after his death people sang of him:

> "Sanctus Ivo erat Brito,
> Advocatus sed non latro:
> Res miranda populo."

In 1285 Ivo was nominated by his bishop to the charge of the parish of Tedrez. It was presumed of course that he would install a salaried curate and he himself dispose of the revenues, this being the custom prevalent in those days. But not so St. Ivo. He spent some time still in his judicial duties, but finding the two offices were incompatible with the time at his disposal, he surrendered his legal work, and after 1288 confined all his energies to the care of his parish. He worked at Tedrez until the bishop appointed him to the larger one of Louannec in 1293, and here he laboured until his death in 1302. Not even St. John Vianney is a better example of a model pastor than the great Breton Curé. For all time St. Ivo stands forth as the ideal of a parish priest. Knowing that an ounce of example is worth a ton of precept, he began to teach his parishioners through his personal holiness.

He continued and even accentuated his habits of mortification both in regard to food and sleep. When not fasting on bread and water, which he seems to have been doing more often than not, he contented himself with the coarsest and most unappetising food. When circumstances required him to dine with the bishop who could ill afford to dispense with the advice of the wisest priest in France, the saint would drown his small portion of wine in water, and would pretend to peck at a little meat or fish, all the while covering up his abstemiousness with entertaining conversation.

His own house became the home of the sick and poor, and his money might be said to have belonged to those in want. At his table all were welcome, rich and poor alike. He always insisted on washing the hands of his guests and took part in serving the food.

He also took a great delight in himself carrying food and other alms to those too infirm to come to him.

In his spiritual ministry St. Ivo was in all things the model pastor. He was most assiduous in tending the sick and administering to them the sacraments, and his devotion to the confessional was very marked. He was most careful about the teaching of the truths of faith to children and to the ignorant, and every Sunday preached to his people at a period when such a duty was too often disregarded. His flock listened with wonder to the simplicity of his discourses which they did not expect from so learned a man; and, he was not content merely to instruct, he rebuked in unmeasured terms all manner of vice; and amidst all the wonderful miracles he wrought in life, none of them equalled the success of his earnest preaching.

The saint received supernatural warning of his approaching death, and on Ascension Day, 1303, celebrated Mass for the last time, supported by other priests, and then, weak as he was, insisted on crawling to the confessional for the last time. In the presence of the vicar-general and many of the canons of the diocesan chapter he received the last Sacraments, lying on a rough bed made of bundles of twigs. His death occurred on May 19, 1303, and his canonization took place in 1347. The Bollandists have published the Acts of this process, together with the sworn testimony of over one hundred and thirty witnesses, amongst whom was the Duke of Brittany himself, John de Montfort, who testified on oath that once he had been given up as lost by physicians during a certain illness, but had been completely restored to health on invoking the saint.

Ivo's life is based on the contemporary and very full biography of the Breton Dominican, Maurice Geoffrey, which is printed in full by the Bollandists, who, by the way, contest the Franciscan claim to number Ivo amongst their tertiaries. Certainly none of the contemporary accounts support this claim.

Acta SS., t. 17 (May 19), pp. 538-614; May 19; Holweck, pp. 515, 516; Thurston's Butler, May.

20.   BLESSED BURCHARD,

Parish Priest of Beinwil in Switzerland.   Early fourteenth century.

SOMETIME after the opening of the fourteenth century died Blessed Burchard, parish priest of Beinwil in Switzerland. The facts of his life have not been preserved, only his cult is remembered. Particular veneration has always been paid to his relics, and indulgences granted by various popes to those visiting his tomb were confirmed and extended by Paul V and subsequent Roman Pontiffs. When the celebration of his feast was definitely transferred to Monday after the Ascension, Pope Clement X (1670-1676) gave permission for the indulgences also to be gained on that day. In the diocese of Basle his feast is now kept on June 27.

Amongst the many miracles, which even up to the beginning of the eighteenth century attested his sanctity, were not a few cases of paralysis. On

April 20, 1645, a youth named Matthias Kaufmann
was cured of what seems to have been a severe
attack of infantile paralysis. The miracle took
place at the tomb of the saint and was attested by
many witnesses. A year previous to this saw the
cure of the paralysed Erhard de Buttisholz who had
vowed, if healed, to go on foot to the saint's shrine.

Acta SS., t. 40 (Aug. 16), pp. 827-32; Holweck, p. 175.

21. BLESSED JOHN,

Parish Priest in Venice. Died about 1348.

BEYOND the fact that Blessed John lived and died
holily, and was parish priest of the church of
St. John Baptist Beheaded (San Giovanni Decollato)
in Venice, we know nothing of him. Even the
suggested date of his death, 1348, is mostly
conjecture. His cult was approved in 1400 by
Boniface IX in interesting circumstances. The
Benedictine nuns of the abbey of St. Lawrence
discovered his relics in a chapel in the abbey church
dedicated to St. Sebastian, from a wonderful perfume
exhaling from a neglected and almost forgotten tomb.
This manifestation was accompanied by a vision of
the saint to one of the nuns and when eventually the
tomb was opened an incorrupt body, clad in the
vestments of a priest, was revealed to the astonished
gaze of the nuns. Naturally enough they began to pay
the saint special devotion, but when this reached
the ears of the bishop he showed "incredulity and
even contempt" (according to the words of

Boniface IX in the bull confirming the saint's cult),
and ordered the relics to be placed in a far less
honourable spot than they were.   An excruciating
pain in his arm, which came on suddenly, made the
prelate rather nervous, and he was converted soon
afterwards to the nuns' view.   He even joined in the
petition requesting the Pope to allow the veneration.
The remains of Blessed John, together with those of
Blessed Leo Bembo, were richly enshrined in 1644.
On the occasion of this translation an interesting
miracle is related of the saint's intervention by
which two little boys who had scrambled up on to a
rather rickety wall were preserved from harm when
it crashed to the ground, just the sort of miracle, in
fact, one would expect of a kindly parish priest.

Acta SS., t. 36 (Aug. 9), pp. 475-82; Holweck, p. 555.

22. ST. JOHN NEPOMUCENE,

Parish Priest of St. Gall in Prague.   Martyr for the seal of Confession.   Died 1393.

SOME exception may be taken to the inclusion of
    this glorious martyr amongst canonized parish
priests, on the ground that he was not a resident
pastor, but spent his years as parish priest of St.
Gall, 1381 to 1389, at the university of Prague, in
the study of jurisprudence in which he graduated as
doctor in 1387.   But there is proof that he did act as
a resident parish priest; and moreover he was
known as the city's greatest preacher.   In 1389 he
surrendered his parish on being appointed vicar

general of the diocese, but he still continued his priestly ministry in the cathedral, especially the duty of preaching. For resisting the encroachments of the Emperor Wenceslaus, who was also King of Bohemia, on the ecclesiastical power, and also for refusing to divulge the secrets of the confessional, St. John was thrown, bound hand and foot, into the river Moldau on the night of March 20, 1393.

The story as told by his contemporaries makes no reference to the seal of confession. They content themselves with the statement that John was slain for resisting the unlawful demands of the king in ecclesiastical matters, just as our own glorious St. Thomas suffered under Henry II. It was not until fifty years after his death that the other reason of his martyrdom was made public. The story as told by Thomas Ebendorfer in 1449 is that the emperor, although passionately devoted to his wife, was himself frequently unfaithful to his marriage vows; and as so often happens in such cases, could not believe in his wife's virtue, although Joan was a woman of remarkable sanctity. He therefore attempted by promises of favours, then by threats followed by torture, to extort from her confessor, St. John, the secrets of her confessions. Whilst the saint was being mercilessly tormented on the rack the emperor himself, we are told, held a lighted torch to his side. St. John Nepomucene was venerated from the day of his martyrdom, but his solemn canonization did not take place until 1729. He is the principal patron of Bohemia.

Acta SS., t. 16 (May 16), pp. 663-76; Holweck, pp. 538, 539; Thurston's Butler, May 16.

23. ST. JOHN OF SAHUGUN, O.S.A.,

Parish Priest of Salamanca.   Died 1479.

ALTHOUGH he did not die a parish priest but as
prior of the Augustinian Hermits in Salamanca,
St. John of Sahugun merits inclusion here on
account of the high degree of sanctity he reached
during his life as a pastor of souls; and even as an
Augustinian he continued in his active ministry.

St. John was educated to be a priest and when
he was still only a boy his father procured for him
the parish of Dornillos, near to the family home at
Sahugun.   The Bishop of Burgos took him into his
own household and ordained him in 1445, after
bestowing upon him several benefices and prebends.
Moreover, as soon as John was a priest the bishop
made him a canon of the cathedral.   The prelate
pointed out to the saint that these livings singly were
not sufficient to live on, and thus excused the
plurality in which the new canon was expected to
live.   But the young man's conscience became
alarmed and he forced the bishop to accept his
resignation of all but the small parish of St. Agatha
which he assiduously tended.   To improve his
theological knowledge he next obtained permission
to go to the university of Salamanca for a four years
course of study, after which he received the
doctorate.   Whilst studying he took charge of the
small parish of St. Sebastian, and continued to serve
this for nine years.   He resided all this time with a
canon named Peter Sancius, himself much revered
by the people for his sanctity.   Here John lived a

most mortified and busy life, but so wore himself out by his work and his austerities that he became gravely ill, and underwent a dangerous operation for the stone.   This was in 1463 and after his recovery he decided to give himself up still more to Almighty God by taking the vows of religion.

He sought and obtained an entry into the convent of the Augustinian Hermits in the city (Salamanca) and made his profession in 1464.   After a few years he was appointed master of novices, and in 1471 was chosen prior.   As an Augustinian he continued his zealous labour for souls, chiefly in the pulpit and the confessional.   Miraculously endowed with discernment he often warned sacrilegious penitents of their crime, and brought them to true penance.   In the pulpit he forgot all human respect for any one sinning, whatever his rank in society.   A wealthy man hired assassins to prevent his speaking out on the oppression of the poor.   When he severely rebuked the immodest dress of women, irate females waylaid him and pelted him with filth and stones; and finally when he persuaded a young man to give up his unlawful companion the evil woman is said to have compassed the saint's death by poison in 1479.   This last statement however, although it was related within a few years of his death, does not appear in his earliest biography.   John of Sahugun was solemnly beatified in 1601 and canonized in 1691.   He is the principal patron of Salamanca, the city in which he so gloriously lived and died.   His feast is kept on June 12.

Acta SS., t. 23 (June 12), pp. 112-57; Holweck, p. 540; Thurston's Butler, June 12.

CHAPTER III

The Later Ages

24. BLESSED JOHN HAILE,

Parish Priest of Isleworth. Died 1535.

BLESSED JOHN HAILE, martyred under Henry VIII on May 4, 1535, was solemnly beatified by Pope Leo XIII on December 29, 1886. He had long been a priest having, it is stated, been nominated parish priest of Chelmsford as far back as 1492. Thirty-one years later he was presented to the parish of Isleworth, then called Thistleworth, in Middlesex, on August 13, 1521. When Henry VIII openly took his mistress Anne Boleyn as his legal wife, and had her crowned queen, John Haile—he is sometimes called Hale or Hall—spoke his mind on the matter in no measured terms to his companions. But in those days of tyranny few confidants could be trusted. Even professed friends were often private enemies and paid spies. In some way the knowledge of the old parish priest's indignation reached government circles, and he was marked down to form one of the first band of priests and religious with whom Henry determined to make a bloody example to the whole realm.

He was accordingly arrested early in 1535 and at the end of April condemned to die a traitor's death in company with four others, namely, three

Carthusian priors, Blessed John Houghton of London, Blessed Augustine Webster of Axholme in Lincolnshire, and Blessed Robert Lawrence of Beauvale in Nottinghamshire, and the Bridgettine monk of Sion, Blessed Richard Reynolds.   These glorious protomartyrs of the English persecutions, were dragged on hurdles to Tyburn Tree and put to death with all the abominable atrocities which attended the English legal punishment of treason.

It was thus that the parish clergy supplied the most venerable of these five martyrs in the person of Blessed John Haile who must have been in his seventieth year or more.

***

Bede Camm, O.S.B., *Lives of the English Martyrs,* London, 1904, pp. 17-26; Gillow's *Biographical Dict. of English Catholics,* London, 1887, vol. iii, p. 88; Stanton's *Menology,* p. 196.

25. BLESSED JOHN LARKE,
Parish Priest of Chelsea.   Died 1545.

BLESSED JOHN LARKE was also a man advanced in years when called upon to give his life for the faith. As early as 1504 he was appointed to the small parish of St. Ethelburga in Bishopsgate, and held this living until within a few years of his death. He became rector of Woodford in Essex in 1526, and in 1530 moved to Chelsea, of which parish he was given charge by the Bishop of London on the presentation of the Lord Chancellor, St. Thomas More. It is due to this appointment that Blessed John is styled by some writers the chaplain of St.

Thomas. In point of fact he was St. Thomas's own parish priest, actually the parish priest of his own choosing. And it is this choice of the chancellor that witnesses to Blessed John's excellence as a priest.

It would of course be Blessed John's Mass that St. Thomas was accustomed to serve, and there is proof that they had a very great esteem for each other, and that his saintly parishioner's martyrdom was taken by John Larke as a premonition of his own in the near future. We have to remember that the oath of Succession, which implicitly denied the papal supremacy, was not offered to all priests, but only to such as the government suspected of denying the king's usurped authority in a public place or manner. Blessed John knew however that the supreme test of his faith could not long be deferred, and less than nine years after St. Thomas's death he was himself butchered at Tyburn on March 7, 1545, for having, so the indictment ran, *been guilty of treason against the king in the matter of his title of supreme head of the Church in England, by his words, writings and acts.* As Blessed John Larke shared in St. Thomas More's martyrdom, so he also shared in his glory, being beatified on the same day, December 29, 1886.

Bede Camm, ibid, pp. 541-3; Holweck, p. 550; Stanton's *Menology*, pp. 107, 108; Gillow, iv, pp. 134, 135.

26-32. THE MARTYRS OF GORCUM.

OF the priests and religious who suffered death in hundreds at the hands of the German, English, Dutch, French, Swiss, Bohemian and Scandinavian Protestants, during the course of the sixteenth century, none have obtained greater renown than the nineteen martyrs of Gorcum, who were solemnly canonized on June 29, 1867, by Pope Pius IX in the presence of three hundred bishops from all parts of the world, gathered together in Rome to celebrate the eighteenth centenary of the martyrdom of the Princes of the Apostles SS. Peter and Paul. It was one of the most glorious canonizations on record, and amongst the nineteen martyrs then raised to the altars were seven parish priests, Leonard Wechel, Nicholas Janssen, Godfrey van Duynen and Andrew Wouters, secular priests, Adrian van Hilvarenbeck and James Lacop, Norbertine Canons, and John of Cologne, a Dominican. All these martyrs, that is the seven parish priests, eleven Franciscans and a Canon Regular of St. Augustine, were arrested, treated with almost satanic fury by their guards and finally done to death by hanging in an empty barn outside the town of Briel in Holland on July 9, 1572. Their murderers were the Calvinist Gueux, or Sea-Beggars, of whose abominable crimes this was but one example. The martyrs were all offered their lives and liberty on condition that they denied the Real Presence and rejected the Papal Supremacy.

E

26. ST. LEONARD WECHEL,

Parish Priest of Gorcum.

ST. LEONARD WECHEL was born at Bois-le-Duc in Holland about the year 1527 and studied at the university of Louvain where he graduated as bachelor in divinity.   The parish of Gorcum in Holland chanced to be vacant at the time he had finished his course, and it was at once offered to him, largely through the influence of Ruard Tapper, the Chancellor of Louvain.   The charge was a heavy one for heresy had made great strides in the district of Gorcum, but the new parish priest was a living saint.   He settled down at once to correct abuses, against two of which he made much headway.   The first was the evil custom that had grown up of espoused couples living together as husband and wife before the marriage ceremony; the second was the custom of inviting heretic relations to stand as godparents in baptism.

His almsgiving was on a big scale, for he himself and his curate, St. Nicholas Janssen, lived so sparingly that much was at their disposition in the matter of charity.   Yet in spite of all his charity his very goodness raised him up many enemies and frequently the windows of his presbytery were smashed by infuriated heretics.   He tried every means to convert these poor souls, and when any one of them was dying he would leave nothing untried to bring him back to God in his last extremity.   He would implore him on his knees not to go out from life unabsolved and unstrengthened by the Holy Viaticum.   In this way he brought many to repent.

Hearing of the approach of the infamous Gueux, his sister came from Bois-le-Duc bidding him fly and hide himself from the coming fury, but he gently though firmly refused to abandon his post. With the Franciscans and other clergy of Gorcum, including his own coadjutor, St. Nicholas, he was arrested and died gloriously on July 9, 1572.

Acta SS., t. 29 (July 9), pp. 736-847; Thurston's Butler, July 9; *Verae effigies Martyrum Gorcomiensium*, by John Boner, O.F.M., Bois-le-Duc, 1623, pp. 52-61. The first two references apply to all the martyrs who follow.

27. ST. NICHOLAS JANSSEN, or POPPEL,

Coadjutor Parish Priest of Gorcum.

THE biographers of the Gorcum martyrs generally call him Poppel after his second surname, instead of Janssen. He was born at Weerd in Holland and carried out both his humanities and his ecclesiastical studies at the university of Louvain. It was here that he made the acquaintance of St. Leonard Wechel, who asked him to come and help him at Gorcum. At first Nicholas acted as curate, but soon was raised by St. Leonard to the post of coadjutor, and they took charge of the parish in alternate weeks. That is the explanation why in the acts of his martyrdom and in his pictures St. Nicholas is styled *parochus secundarius Gorcumiensis*. This does not mean that only one of these saints did parish work during the week, but that one was made the responsible pastor for that

particular period. St. Nicholas for some time enter-
tained the wish to enter the Society of Jesus; but St.
Leonard persuaded him that the parish of Gorcum
needed him, as holy priests were then wanted more
than ever.   This was but one more case of a holy
man fearing the cares of a parish weigh too heavy
upon him, and at the same time, so conscious of his
own unworthiness as a labourer that he desired to
retire into religion.

Another temptation to leave Gorcum came from
his father who knew the danger his son was in
whilst working there. But this temptation had no
subtlety for him. His outstanding devotion was to
the Blessed Sacrament of the Altar and all that
redounded to Its honour. He was arrested with St.
Leonard and martyred with his eighteen companions
on July 9, 1572.

Boner, ibid, pp. 61-67; Holweck, p. 740.

28. ST. GODFREY VAN DUYNEN,

formerly in charge of a small parish on the French frontier.

THIS Flemish saint was living in retirement in his
native town of Gorcum when it was seized by
the heretics, and he with the other clergy of the place
fell into the hands of the persecutors. At this time
Saint Godfrey was about seventy years of age
incapable of any priestly work but saying Mass and
reciting his Office. As a young man he studied in
the university of Paris, and was placed over a school

in that city. He held this post for some years and was then persuaded to become a priest. After his ordination he was given charge of a small parish on the Belgian and French border, but none of his biographers name the place.

He was of a nervous and scrupulous disposition, and through excessive and imprudently conducted meditations his brain became affected. Quite evidently he had not heard the wise words of his saintly fellow countryman the Abbot Blosius in the 24th chapter of *The Paradise of the Faithful Soul*: "Be careful not to lay upon thy weak shoulders too heavy a weight, lest, oppressed and overpowered by the burden, thou shouldst be forced to faint and give way. Even in tears of devotion a measure should be observed, *lest the head be weakened,* especially if those tears are accompanied by strong emotion."

Eventually this affection of the head became so severe that he was forced to resign his living, for he was incapable of further active work.

Much is told of his sanctity, but although a great saint he was no more exempt than the other sons of Adam from temptations against holy purity. We read in his life that if these attacked him at night he would immediately rise and throw himself on his knees, praying God most earnestly to prevent him falling into temptation. William Est, the contemporary historian of the martyrs of Gorcum, relates how Saint Godfrey cured the eye trouble of Rutger, William's brother. Rutger was serving his Mass and the saint dipped his finger into the contents of the chalice after the second ablutions, and anointed the diseased eyes, which immediately were healed.

When Saint Godfrey was being led to execution with his companions, one of the bystanders out of a motive of kindness called to the soldiers that the old priest was weak in the head, and it would be a shameful thing to put such a one to death.   The cruel reply was: "If he has got head enough to say Mass, he has got head enough to be hanged".   Saint Godfrey suffered with the other eighteen martyrs on July 9, 1572, crying aloud as he was being hanged that he saw the heavens opened to receive the martyred band.

Boner, pp. 68-71.

29. ST. ANDREW WOUTERS,

Parish Priest of Heinort.

IN this canonized parish priest we find a very different character from the preceding. As parish priest of Heinort near Dortrecht in Holland, his unchaste life was an open scandal. And yet in His infinite mercy God turned Andrew's heart so that in his last hours on earth he became a chosen vessel. Arrested by the Gueux, he stoutly professed his faith and was carried to Briel to be tortured and slain with the rest. And with them he died gloriously on July 9, 1572, and shared in the glory of their canonization.

On the other hand Est tells us that the parish priest of Maesdam—charitably he refuses to give the man's name—being promised pardon, denied his priesthood, the Papal Supremacy and the whole Catholic faith, and moreover solemnly promised never to return to these beliefs.   His brutal tormentors, having thus got him to deny Christ, immediately hanged him in the place to which they had carried him apart from the rest. This occurred eight days after the great martyrdom. Est adds that this priest though of good life was very unlettered. A canon of Gorcum also wavered, but on being liberated some time later, returned to the faith and died a good Catholic.

Acta SS., t. 29, pp. 820-2; Holweck, p. 71.

30.   ST. JOHN OF COLOGNE, O.P.,
Parish Priest of Hornar.

SAINT JOHN received his surname either because he was born, or took the Dominican habit at Cologne. We know nothing at all of his life beyond the fact that, touched by the destitution of the Dutch Catholics consequent on the death of so many priests at the hands of the Calvinists, he begged leave from his superiors to go to their aid. The permission was granted and he was given charge of the parish of Hornar not far from Gorcum; and when the clergy of the latter place were arrested John came privately to administer to the Catholics now deprived of the Sacraments. His arrest took place when going to Gorcum to baptise a newly born infant, and he was thrown into the same gaol which held the eleven Franciscan saints and the parochial clergy already

mentioned, with the exception of Saint Andrew
Wouters not yet seized by the heretics.

Saint John after sharing in the exquisite tortures
to which the brave Gorcum band of martyrs were
subjected, died for his faith along with the rest on
July 9, 1572.

Année Dominicaine, Lyons, 1895, t. 7, pp. 195-208; *Short
Lives of Dominican Saints*, ed. Procter, London, 1901.

31.   ST. ADRIAN HILVARENBECK,

Norbertine Canon, Parish Priest of Munster in Holland.

THE parish of Munster, a town of Holland near the
mouth of the Meuse, was in the gift of the
Norbertine, or Premonstratensian, Abbey of Middelburg, and at the time of the Gorcum martyrdom was
being administered by a saintly canon of that abbey,
Adrian Becanus, better known as Hilvarenbeck
from the place of his birth in Brabant.   He had
entered the Order in 1557, and after twenty-five
years in the cloister was appointed to Munster early
in 1572.   He was a man of wholly admirable life and
did all that lay in his power to stir up the zeal of his
flock in the service of God, and in this was greatly
assisted by his curate, Saint James Lacop.   Both
were captured on July 7 by the Gueux and led to
join the other martyrs at Briel.   Saint Adrian closed
his holy career with his companions on July 9, 1572.

32. ST. JAMES LACOP,

Norbertine Canon, Curate to St. Adrian.

SAINT JAMES LACOP was born at Oudenarde and entered the abbey of Middelburg, from which he apostatized in 1566.   He was an engaging youth both in appearance and manners, and was much spoiled in consequence.   Even as a young religious he used frequently to speak slightingly of his Order and of the Church, thinking youth-like he was being broad-minded.   The defection of so unbalanced a religious, whilst it greatly grieved his brethren, cannot have caused them over much astonishment.

On his apostasy he joined himself with the Calvinists, preached openly against the faith, and went so far as to publish a small book in mockery of the well-known medieval collection of the lives of the Saints that went under the name of the *Golden Legend*. No one would seriously have objected had Lacop confined himself merely to criticism of so ancient a work on the grounds of its historical inaccuracy, but his attack was malicious.

All this, we must confess, was but a poor preparation for the martyr's crown, which however in a short six years from his apostasy he was destined to gain.   A few months in the company of the heretics was more than enough to disgust him, and, receiving from God the wonderful grace to repent, returned to his abbey, publicly confessed his crime against God and his own brethren, and in their presence consigned his infamous book to the flames.

Cheerfully and even joyously he underwent penance for his lapse; and his superiors, to make things more pleasant for him, and incidentally to lessen the scandal he had caused in the vicinity of Middelburg, sent him to another abbey in Flanders. Shortly afterwards he was appointed to assist his own brother, Adrian Lacop, also a Norbertine, in the administration of the parish of Munster, and on his brother's death remained as curate to the new parish priest, Saint Adrian Hilvarenbeck, with whom he was arrested and in whose company he died on July 9, 1572. At the hour of death the heretics threw in his face his former apostasy, and urged him to recant once again; but he replied that with the help of God he would suffer any torment rather than consent.

33. BLESSED JOHN SARKANDER,

Parish Priest of Holleschau in Moravia.   Died 1620.

IN Blessed John Sarkander we find a martyr of the confessional comparable to Saint John Nepomucene. He was born in Austrian Silesia in 1576, and was ordained priest in 1607 after doing his studies in the university of Prague. In 1613 he was given charge of the parish of Boskowitz, but in 1616, at the earnest request of his influential penitent, Baron Popel of Lobkowitz, governor of Moravia, he was appointed parish priest of Holleschau in that province.

One of the local lords, Bitowsky of Bistriz, a

fierce Protestant, hated Baron Popel and turned his hatred in consequence on to Blessed John, the favourite of the governor. Bitowsky was particularly furious at the many reconciliations to the Church brought about by the new pastor's zealous preaching, and so great was his violence against the Catholic Faith that John judged it prudent for a time to withdraw to Cracow. But he did not absent himself long, and in a few months was back at his post as busy as ever in trying to stem the tide of heresy; and with extraordinary success.

As so often happens, however, when good is being done the devil stirred up political troubles in which to ensnare the nations to the detriment of Catholicism, and too often Catholics are themselves to blame. Thus it chanced at this time that the Poles, going to the assistance of the emperor of Germany, passed through Moravia pillaging as they went this very Protestant province. At the prayers of Blessed John they spared Holleschau the horrors of a sack, but instead of gratitude John was met with hatred by those for whom he had obtained this boon. Bitowsky called upon his countrymen to witness this actual sparing of Holleschau by the Poles, as a proof that John was implicated in the invasion; and personally accused him of inviting the Poles into the country. He even had him arrested and inhumanly tortured to force him to reveal what Baron Popel had told him in confession; for to Popel was assigned the chief share in the supposed invitation.

The saint refused all knowledge of the coming of the Poles, and refused to listen to the reiterated demands of his torturers that he should reveal the secrets of the confessional, although he was most horribly tormented on the rack by having his sides burnt with torches. Twice this frightful punishment was inflicted, but he remained indomitable. Furious at his refusal his maddened tormenters covered him from head to foot with feathers steeped in fat, pitch, oil and sulphur and then set his body ablaze. Incredible though it may seem, Blessed John survived even this fiendish torture and lingered in great agony for another month, lying on the floor of his dungeon. Strange to say he was not forbidden the last Sacraments, and having received these he joyfully died on March 17, 1620. In 1859 Pope Pius IX declared him Blessed and permission was granted by the Holy See for his feast to be kept throughout Moravia and Bohemia. His body is preserved in the cathedral at Olmutz.

Holweck, pp. 550, 551; Thurston's Butler, March 17; Catholic Encyclopedia.

34. ST. PETER FOURIER,
Canon Regular. Parish Priest of Mattaincourt.
Died 1640.

ON more than one count Saint Peter Fourier can claim to be, with the exception only of St. John Vianney, the best example of a canonized parish priest, seeing that he held that office for thirty-eight years, namely from 1594 to 1632, that in it he found his sanctification, that the ecclesiastical authorities were agreed in regarding him as the ideal of a parish priest, and that he has always been known as "the good pastor of Mattaincourt". Towards the end of his long life he began a little treatise on "the duties of a parish priest" which either was never completed, or partly lost, for his biographer and disciple Père Bedel was not able to discover more than twenty pages, all of which he incorporated into his life of the saint. St. Jane Frances de Chantal, who knew him well, wrote: "It suffices to see the holy rector of Mattaincourt, to esteem him as a saint".

Saint Peter was born at Mirecourt in Lorraine in 1565 and at the age of nineteen sought and obtained admission into the Abbey of Chaumousey lying among the Vosges Mountains and belonging since the eleventh century to the Canons Regular of St. Augustine. Four years later, on September 14, 1588, he was ordained priest, but continued his theological studies in the Jesuit university of Pont-a-Mousson until 1594. This long absence is only to be explained by the laxity prevailing in the abbey, a state of things that had caused Peter intense grief all through the time of his probation. But it had never made him falter in his resolution to persevere. At Pont-a-Mousson, however, he found real holiness of life amongst the Jesuits and his brethren at the abbey seemed well content to have him at a distance.

In 1594 he was at length recalled and given charge of the parish attached to the abbey. Perhaps the canons thought this post would fill up his time so that he would have little left to spend in the monastery, there to reproach by his observance of the rule their own negligence.

But his life still constituted an offence to them and

they offered him his choice of three parishes in the abbey's gift; and after consulting a Jesuit, his uncle Father Fourier, he accepted Mattaincourt, a flourishing town in a fold of the Vosges. He went to his new parish in 1597 and found it contaminated with Protestantism and morally rotten, but he held to his task until 1632 when he was elected superior of that branch of his Order which he had been instrumental in reforming, whilst still in residence at Mattaincourt. In fact he only left Mattaincourt in 1636 driven out as an exile for his loyalty to his dispossessed prince, the Duke of Lorraine; and he died an exile on December 9, 1640.

Saint Peter Fourier's career is thus an inversion of a not uncommon order of things in which we read of parish priests entering a religious Order for the greater sanctification of their souls. Peter was driven by a desire of greater sanctification to become a parish priest, despairing otherwise of obtaining that holiness of life of which he was robbed in the cloister, and so his life may justly be considered the complete reply to those who in Ghéon's words, consider ''that there is no condition in the whole world in which sanctity is more difficult to attain'' than in the position of parish priest.

Peter's coming to Mattaincourt reminds us of John Vianney's coming to Ars. Morally, we have said, the place was rotten, with impurity its chief vice; and the church was in an almost ruinous condition. But a material building can soon be repaired —a ruined people take longer to rise again. Peter however set to, with a will, and after his pastorate of thirty-five years the face of the place was changed.

Yet it had cost him much; and many were the attacks on him. Once a young libertine from whom Peter had saved a young woman beat him unmercifully the whole length of the town. On another occasion an abandoned woman tried to obstruct his passage through a narrow road when he was actually carrying the Blessed Sacrament. Unhesitating the saint waded through a foul pool of water at the road-side, "thus choosing of two mires the least infectious", wrote Pope Clement XI during the preliminary process of his beatification. However, in the end all opposition ceased, Mattaincourt no longer deserved its reproachful name of "little Geneva", and the saint and reformer became "the good father of Mattaincourt".

His success was undoubtedly due to his affection for his people. "You can never know," he wrote to a friend, "the depth of love a priest bears to his children until you become one yourself. All the similes made use of, such as a mother and her children, a hen and her chickens, seem to me to fall far short of reality; nor have I ever read any work on this subject which says half enough of it. Experience alone can tell the truth of what I say."

As a parish priest he never forgot his religious status, and his monastic poverty was kept with the most scrupulous exactitude. All money he received he looked upon as a sacred trust for the parish and the poor. He instituted a fund known as St. Evre's purse, in memory of the patron saint of the town St. Evre or Aper, Bishop of Toul in the year 500. Into this fund went all gifts and bequests, and from it he advanced small sums up to a few hundred francs as loans to tradesmen involved in temporary difficulties, stipulating for repayment only in the event of their again flourishing in business.

For the furtherance of good morals he instituted three confraternities, that of St. Sebastian for the men, the Rosary for women and that of the Immaculate Conception for girls.   To better the state of Christian education he established an institute of nuns called Canonesses Regular of St. Augustine of Notre Dame, and gave them charge of his free schools for girls.   When the numbers of these religious women increased, so that branch houses were founded, the saint obtained papal confirmation of his new Order from Pope Urban VIII.   With his project for the education of boys he failed, for although he tried to get together some young men whom he could train as schoolmasters, he had no success.   This work was reserved for the great saint, John Baptist de la Salle, a quarter of a century later.

In his own person St. Peter Fourier showed such an example of holiness and mortification that the parish entrusted to him could not but be edified. His life was one of wonderful austerity.   He never used a fire for himself—it was only lighted when he had guests.   His bed was nothing but an ornament in his poor bedroom.   It was never slept in, but a hard and narrow bench next to it was his couch.   As he spent so little on himself he had quite a useful balance to spend on the poor; but the scale on which he helped them would have been impossible without frequent miracles, and that these were frequent his canonization process fully proves.

Whilst still at Mattaincourt he was commissioned

by the Holy See to visit and reform all the houses of his Order in the diocese of Toul, and when this was completed he was chosen superior-general of these same houses now formed by authority from Rome into the congregation of Our Saviour. This choice was made in 1632 and Peter at once appointed another Canon Regular to succeed him at Mattaincourt. Bitter trials now tested the old priest. In 1636 he was driven into exile by Richelieu for his fidelity to the house of Lorraine, and he found a refuge at Gray in Franche Comté, but died four years later still an outcast from his country on December 9, 1640.

But his death was a marvellous scene of joy after all his sorrows, as he lay pressing the crucifix to his lips, begging pardon for his offences, frequently breaking out into the words, "Monstra te esse matrem", and spending long periods in thanksgiving, apparently rapt in ecstasy.

After his death his body was first interred at Gray, but later it was taken to Mattaincourt where a magnificent shrine was erected over the holy remains. In 1730 Peter Fourier was solemnly beatified by Pope Benedict XIII, and canonized by Pope Leo XIII in 1897.

His life was first written by his disciple and companion Père Bedel. Other lives by Hazelaire, trans. into English by G. White, 1860, and Vuillimin, 1897. See also *Dictionnaire Universelle*, by Richard, Paris, new edition 1822, t. 11, pp. 257, 258, and Thurston's Butler, July 7.

35. ST. JOHN BAPTIST ROSSI,
Canon of S. Maria in Cosmedin in Rome.
(1698-1764)

SAINT JOHN BAPTIST ROSSI although never in complete charge of a parish is included in this book on the grounds that he held a benefice, and later a canonry, attached to the church of S. Maria in Cosmedin at the foot of the Aventine Hill, and there ministered to the surrounding people for thirty-two years. The additional work he did in Rome for the sick and the poor, fallen women and prisoners, the ill-instructed labourers in the city and peasants from the Campagna, has tended to eclipse the memory of his main pre-occupation of ministering to those who came under his direct care in the district round his church.

Born at Voltaggio in the diocese of Genoa in 1698, one of a family of four children, he was remarkable as a child not merely for his piety but the gift he possessed of inspiring his playmates with some of his own fervour, a gift he continued to exercise when he was a youth at the Roman College and which was the secret of his future success with all classes during the forty-three years of his priestly career. In 1708 a well-to-do couple from Genoa came to spend the summer at Voltaggio and being struck by the good qualities and charm of this boy of ten begged his parents to let them take charge of his further education. The saint accompanied them back to Genoa where he attracted the attention of the Capuchins who reported most favourably of him to their Provincial who was his uncle, who however seems to have made no suggestion that his nephew should enter the same Order and left it to another relative to turn the boy's thoughts to the sanctuary.

This was his cousin Lorenzo Rossi, a secular priest and canon of S. Maria in Cosmedin, who invited John Baptist to Rome and arranged for his reception into the Roman College where he proved himself an excellent student until ill-health forced him to leave at the end of his classical course. This breakdown seems to have been occasioned by excessive bodily mortification undertaken without the advice of a prudent confessor and after reading some austere treatise on the spiritual life. He never completely regained his health and although he reached his sixty-sixth year and worked as a priest for forty-three he was never entirely free from physical suffering. He did however recover sufficiently to undertake his theological studies in the Dominican college of the Minerva and was ordained priest on March 8, 1721. His first post was in the hospice for the poor at S. Galla and he continued to help there all through his life, and he also assisted later on in the hospital of S. Trinita dei Pellegrini where he died.

For a year or two following his ordination he was afraid to hear confessions but after an illness in the house of Bishop Tenderini of Civita Castellana he was persuaded by that prelate to make a beginning in his diocese and he soon discovered that in the confessional was his true vocation. His words on the subject are memorable. "I often used to wonder what was the shortest road to heaven. It lies in guiding others through the confessional.''

On his return to Rome he early turned his attention to teamsters and cattle-drovers who came daily into the city from the Campagna, and each day early and late he spent hours amongst them instructing them in the faith and preparing them for the sacraments. He was equally zealous for sinners and in 1731, helped by alms from Pope Clement XII and other benefactors, he established a refuge for fallen women driven on to the streets mostly by sheer want. He himself had no money beyond the few alms he received as Mass stipends, but he had a little more to give away after his appointment the same year as assistant priest at S. Maria in Cosmedin through the kind offices of his uncle, Canon Rossi, and when that good priest died in 1736 the chapter of canons elected John Baptist to the vacant canonry. In his love of poverty he would not dwell in the house that went with this appointment and surrendered it to the chapter, and set aside the annual income to help in the expenses of the church for which he provided both an organ and an organist's salary. He himself continued to dwell in a poor attic.

On first coming to S. Maria he found the church services very poorly attended, but his zeal and fervour rapidly made a difference and before long he was kept busy in the confessional for many hours each day. Eventually his penitents required so much of his time that both Clement XII and Benedict XIV dispensed him from the obligation of choral recitation of the divine office to which the clergy of S. Maria were bound, as their church ranked as a collegiate one.   In addition to his fame as a confessor he had a reputation as an excellent preacher and gave many missions in the churches of Rome and also many conferences to religious men and women.

In 1763 he became so weak that he took up his quarters in the hospital of S. Trinita where in December a stroke put an end to his active career and although he rallied sufficiently to be able once more to say Mass the end came on May 23, 1764. He left no money so the hospital had to undertake the expenses of the quiet and extremely poor funeral that was envisaged, but as happens so often at the death of His saints God glorified His beloved servant by a wonderful demonstration of popular devotion. The procession to the church of S. Trinita was attended by two hundred and sixty clergy, numerous religious and a vast concourse of the faithful, whilst the Requiem was celebrated by Archbishop Lercari, vicegerent of Rome, attended by the Papal Choir. The holy remains were buried in the church and there they remain under a side altar.   Many miracles attested his sanctity and this ideal pastor of souls was beatified by Pius IX in 1860 and canonized by his successor Leo XIII in 1881.

Thurston's *Butler,* May 23, pp. 279 seq.; Holweck, p. 539. The earliest life was by J. M. Toretti in 1768 and the latest was by Fr. H. Cormier, in 1901.   Fr. Cormier's own process of beatification is expected to be introduced shortly.

36.   BLESSED NOEL PINOT, Martyr,

Parish Priest of Louroux-Beconnais.   (1747-1794.)

BLESSED NOEL PINOT, one of the greatest
glories of the French priesthood, was guillotined
in his sacred vestments at the height of the fury of
the French Revolution for refusing to take the
iniquitous oath of the Civil Constitution expressly
condemned by the Holy See.

The son of Réné Pinot and his wife Claudia,
née La Grois, Noel was born at Angers on December
19, 1747, and baptised in the church of St. Martin
on the following day.   After his ordination he was
sent as curate to Bouasse until in 1776 he became
assistant to the parish priest at Corzé.   Five years
later he was appointed chaplain to a hospital for
incurables in Angers which was attached to his native
parish of St. Martin.   Finally he was nominated
parish priest of Louroux-Béconnais by the canons of
the chapter of Angers under whose appraising eyes
he must have worked in the episcopal city, for we
are told their choice was unanimous.   This was
in 1788, almost on the eve of the Revolution, but
in the short time afforded him he did much to draw
his people to a true sense of religion and converted
many sinners.

When the king, Louis XVI, was forced by the
National Assembly in 1789 to accept the Civil Constitution of the Clergy, a measure aimed directly at
cutting off the Church in France from union with
Rome, the clergy were commanded to accept an
oath of obedience to this Constitution, an oath

condemned by the Holy See. Blessed Noel was amongst the great number of priests who refused to take it, and after being arrested in Angers was brought before a revolutionary tribunal and sentenced to be banished from his parish for two years, a sentence he defied by working in secret; and he encouraged his brother priests to do the same. In 1794 the initial success of the revolt in La Vendée seemed to herald a dawn of peace for France and Noel took advantage of it to appear once more openly in his parish and conducted services in his church; and even when the patriots were crushed he resumed once more his secret ministry.

Eventually he was betrayed and by a man to whom he had shown considerable kindness. Seized when actually vested for Mass he was dragged through the streets in his sacred vestments amidst a jeering mob of soldiers and "citizens", and still clad in his vestments thrown into prison where he was roughly handled and treated with great cruelty to force him to take the oath. After repeated refusals he was taken from prison after twelve days and carried off to the guillotine still robed for Mass and on his way recited the psalm: Introibo ad altare Dei. His glorious death took place on February 21, 1794, and he was solemnly beatified by Pius XI on October 31, 1926. His feast was approved for the diocese of Angers. In the same year, Pius XI beatified 191 martyrs of the Revolution, of whom 64 were parochial clergy; too great a number to be dealt with here.

Thurston's Butler, Feb., pp. 297, 298; Acta Apostolicae Sedis, vol. xi, pp. 86-8; vol. xviii, pp. 415-426.

37. ST. ANDREW HUBERT FOURNET,

Parish Priest of Maille near Poitiers. (1752-1834.)

IN all but the actual sacrifice of his life, Saint
Andrew Hubert Fournet lived a life almost
exactly paralleled by that of his contemporary
Blessed Noel Pinot. Like him he was working
zealously in his parish when the Reign of Terror
broke out, and toiled secretly for his distressed flock
whilst the hunters were on his trail, and on at least
two occasions narrowly escaped capture and death.

The son of well-to-do parents Peter Fournet de
Thoiré and Florence Elizabeth, née Chasseloup, of
the little town of Maillé near Poitiers, Andrew was
born there on December 6, 1752, and baptized by
his uncle the parish priest on the following day. His
mother, a very devout woman, wished him to
become a priest but the boy's thoughts did not extend
beyond the playground. He wanted above all to
amuse himself and scribbled in a little exercise book,
now preserved as a relic, "This book belongs to
Andrew Hubert Fournet, a good boy, although he
is not going to be a priest or a monk". Once he
ran away from his detested school but was brought
back and soundly thrashed. As a youth he was
sent to study law at Poitiers but again ran away and
joined the army. His persevering parents bought
him out and packed him off to another priest-uncle
who lived in a poor parish at some distance from
Maillé, and this man entirely won his confidence and
affection so that he willingly embarked on the study

of theology and being ordained remained as curate
to this uncle until he was offered his native parish
of Maillé.

Here he worked with great zeal and was generous
to those in want, but lived himself in some style,
keeping a well-provided table for his friends and
acquaintances.   One day he chanced to overhear a
caustic remark made by one beggar to another and
it rankled, but seeing the justice of it he entered into
himself and determined to live in a fashion that could
cause no scandal.   He sold every bit of his silver
plate and every piece of grand furniture, and gave
the proceeds in charity, after which he lived in
quiet seclusion with his curate in the denuded
presbytery which was kept in order by his mother
and sister who seemingly were pleased to do the
work once performed by a number of servants.
Andrew did not stop at jettisoning his material
wealth, he sacrificed nearly all the fine phrases and
riches of erudition with which he was wont to adorn
his sermons and contented himself with explaining
the Gospel and catechism in the simplest terms.   His
lay sacristan bewailing the loss of those rolling
periods complained bitterly that once the saint used
to preach so well that few understood him but now
it was all too simple.

This tranquil life of parochial activity was rudely
shattered by the onrush of the Revolution and
because in 1790 Andrew refused the Constitutional
Oath he was outlawed and forced to work in secret
carrying his life in his hands, and saying Mass in
disused barns and poor cottages, and even in the
woods where he sometimes dwelt.   After two years

his bishop got a message through to him bidding him withdraw across the Spanish frontier to Los Arcos in Pampeluna, but five years later he risked his life in order to return to his desolated parish.

The news of his arrival was not long in reaching the authorities and the pursuivants were once more hot on his trail.   One evening as he sat dressed in old clothes in front of the fire in a small farm house his pursuers entered to discover information of his whereabouts but their suspicions were lulled when the farmer's wife gave the saint a resounding box on his ear and ordered him to get up and make room for the gentlemen to sit down, and then to betake himself to his work in the cowshed.   He later confessed that the buffet was no mere pretence and that he really did see stars.   On another occasion he outwitted his hunters by shamming dead, lying under a shroud with lighted candles round his bed and with some kneeling women weeping and praying at his side.

In 1801 Napoleon, now in complete control as First Consul, saw France had had enough of revolutionary tyranny and determined to make peace with the Church.   Andrew therefore found himself once more free to take up openly his sacred duties and immediately set about the task of bringing his scattered flock back to a true sense of religion and morality, and was as successful in this as his contemporary St. John Vianney at Ars.   He was greatly helped by Elizabeth Bichier des Ages and her four companions Anne Bernier, Veronica Lavergne, Magdalene Morea and Marie Anne Guillon, who constituted themselves his disciples and eventually formed the Order of the Daughters of the Cross. Under the saint's guidance they devoted themselves to teaching children and nursing the sick poor. Elizabeth, who assumed the name of Jeanne Marie when she took her vows, died in 1838 and was beatified by Pius XI in 1934.

In 1821 when he had reached his sixty-eighth year Andrew was forced by ill-health and great weakness to resign his parish and retired to the mother-house of his nuns the Daughters of the Cross at Puy where he remained until his death thirteen years later, training his daughters in the spiritual life and continuing to minister to souls by hearing confessions and preaching in other churches to help the neighbouring clergy. He also acted as confessor to many of these and numerous layfolk.

His death took place on May 13, 1834, in the eighty-second year of his age, and he was beatified in 1885 by Leo XIII and canonized by Pius XI on June 4, 1933. The acts of his canonization record many miracles including the multiplication of provisions, and sometimes of grain when the nuns of La Puy were without bread for themselves and the children.

Acta Apost. Sed., xxv, 1933, 288, 417-26; L. Rigaud, Vie de A. H. Fournet (1885), La beata Elisabetta Bichier des Ages (1934); Thurston's Butler, May 13, p. 168; Anonymous Life in Italian (1885).

38. ST. JOHN MARY BAPTIST VIANNEY,

Parish Priest of Ars. Died 1859.

THERE is little need here to give more than the merest outline of a life so well known as that of the Curé d'Ars.   He was born at Dardilly, near Lyons, on May 8, 1786, and therefore passed his early boyhood under the revolutionary government, which was also a bitterly persecuting one; so much so that Mass could only be heard in secret and John, when a boy of thirteen, had to receive his first Holy Communion in conditions of great danger.   But the rise of Napoleon to supreme power restored liberty to the Church when John was scarcely another year older.

Although he longed to become a priest John could not be spared from work on his father's farm, and consequently was not able to begin his studies until he had reached his twentieth year.   Eventually he was ordained in 1815 but only after many difficulties due to his poor talent for learning had been almost miraculously overcome;   and was immediately appointed as curate to that uncanonized saint, M. Balley.   After three years in so holy a household John was sent as parish priest to Ars, where he remained until his death forty-one years later.

St. John Mary had one ambition, to renew the faith of the people of Ars and to bring them back into the way of salvation.   He had no intention of converting the world, and his humility would have been hurt by the suggestion that he was fit for any

parish other than his little village. In fact he
refused the much more important one of Fareins
offered him by Bishop Devie, because he honestly
believed that any priest but himself would have more
success in reforming that place, then a stronghold
of Jansenism. Yet in spite of his humility, his work
at Ars had an effect felt far and wide throughout the
whole of France and many other countries. Of him
could be justly said the words of the eighteenth
Psalm, used by the Church in her Office for an
Apostle, *Their sound hath gone forth into all the
earth: and their words unto the ends of the world.*

The conversion of Ars was begun by example no
less than precept; of the two more teaching by
personal sanctity than by word of mouth. His mode
of life bordered on the miraculous, and it is difficult
to understand how he managed with his meagre diet
to keep life in his weak frame, and still more
astonishing to understand how he could have lived
to a comparatively great age, seeing that he had
already entered his seventy-fourth year when he
died. Sometimes it seemed that he almost lived without food. Once when employed in giving a mission at
Montmerle, a parish in the neighbourhood, he had to
lodge out with an excellent Catholic family, whose
only grievance was that the saint preferred to eat at
the presbytery rather than with them. Naturally they
did not complain, as they rightly judged it was more
fitting to his priestly character. The parish priest
on his side regretted that the holy Curé preferred to
take his meals with his kind hosts, and to St. John's
great delight he was able to live the whole weak on
the contents of a small basin of cold potatoes. The

servant of the family, under the promise of secrecy
extorted from her, had helped in this little plot, as
she afterwards confessed to her disappointed
mistress and to the parish priest.

After example came his direct teaching from the
pulpit, and the labour this entailed on a man of so
poor a memory as St. John can scarcely be realised.
All the preparation of his sermons was done in the
little sacristy with the door open on to the chancel,
so that he could glance frequently at the tabernacle.
He wrote page after page, for he nearly always
occupied an hour in preaching, and when all this
labour of writing was finished there remained the
painful toil of trying to commit it to his weak
memory.   There is little to wonder at when we read
of his having frequently to break off his discourse
and come down from the pulpit.   His preaching was
vehement to a degree, and often sheer hoarseness
made him give up.   But his thundering against vice,
Sunday after Sunday, did eventually renew the
whole face of the village.   Abuses ceased, sins
became fewer, and licence entirely disappeared.
Moreover the words spoken in the little village
church echoed far and wide.   Ars was not the world;
it seemed almost out of the world; but the world in a
few years came pouring in.   The pilgrimages of
hundreds who wished to share in the benefits of the
Curé's ministry in pulpit and confessional had
begun, and St. John Mary was no longer just parish
priest of Ars, he was the spiritual director of
thousands in France and in other countries.

Once when he was asked why he raised his voice
so much in preaching but recited the public prayers

softly, he replied that men were sleepy and deaf, God was not. The night of Saturday was often spent in walking about the lanes, reciting his forthcoming sermon aloud, to the no little fright of belated passers-by. He would then return to the church to pray, afterwards sleeping a little on the hard floor of the sacristy. We have to remember that in addition to all this labour over his sermon, he was fasting from Saturday midday until after the 11 o'clock Mass on Sunday, which he himself celebrated and at which he delivered his sermon.

But it is in connection with his work in the confessional that St. John Mary will probably be best remembered in future ages. It was the most marked of all his apostolic labours, and, as we have already said, it extended far and wide beyond Ars. The confessional may truly have been described as his crucifixion, and one of his biographers, the Abbé Monnin, calls him the "martyr of the confessional". The Abbé Trochu describes him as "riveted to that hard seat of his confessional, a prisoner of sinners". One robust curate confessed that one week alone of the work of the confessional as performed by the Curé would have wrecked his health. And yet this was the life of the saint for thirty years.

In his earlier days he was able to spend much time visiting his parishioners in their homes, or taking a little exercise in the beautiful wooded countryside; but in later years attendance in the confessional took up most of his day, summer and winter. The saint once admitted that in summer "the heat of the confessional gave him an idea of hell". As to the winter, he said to a friend, "from

All Saints until Easter I do not feel my feet at all''.
Yet he would never tolerate a foot-warmer, and
when small cushions were sometimes placed on the
hard board on which he sat for so many hours, he
invariably pushed them away.   Towards the end of
his life, his devoted friends found a way of placing
a foot-warmer under the boards of his confessional
floor, and for a long time the trick escaped
unnoticed, but when he did finally discover it, he
allowed it to go on, for he was now so near the
completion of his work for God that he gladly con-
served the little extra energy this gave him.

When we read all this it causes little or no wonder
to be told that rumours occasionally got about that
he had been found dead in his confessional; and
certainly on many occasions he came out from it
almost in a swooning condition.   Once when helping
with confessions in the neighbouring parish church
of Trévoux, so great was the crowd round his confessional that it was nearly upset, a circumstance
that the Curé used afterwards to describe with much
amusement.   Only six days before his death he was
seated in the confessional at one o'clock in the
morning, but this was the final act of his ministry
for souls in the tribunal of penance.   All that morning he heard confessions, though consumed by a
raging fever.   He even attempted to preach, but his
voice was inaudible and he was carried from the
pulpit to his bed, from which he never again rose.
So weak he was that he did not even protest against
their placing a mattress under him, a luxury he had
not enjoyed since first coming to Ars, except in his
terrible illness of the year 1843.   Far from chiding

his friends for this infringement of his lifelong rule, he gently smiled his thanks.

All through his priestly life the Curé was a devoted friend to his priestly brethren, ever ready to help them in sickness or in any other pressing difficulty. If a neighbouring priest were old or ill, St. John Mary was always the first to offer help in taking sick-calls by day or by night. These night journeys were always accomplished on foot, no matter how distant; and although he had frequently to plough his way through snow and deep mud, so that he returned home on the verge of complete exhaustion, he always looked radiantly happy. One of these priests was M. Ducreux, a man of nearly eighty, and another was the Abbé Louis Beau, parish priest of Jassans, a man of great holiness of life and moreover the saint's confessor. To him was given the sorrowful, yet joyful privilege, of administering to the saint the last Sacraments. Only at the bidding of charity did the Curé leave his own parish, and even when he occasionally assisted in giving missions in other parishes, he returned home at night if physically possible; and his idea of what was physically possible was bigger than that of most priests. Thus, for example, when helping in a mission at Trévoux during one January, he walked back each night to Ars, six miles distant.

If his charity to his distant neighbours was so great, we can measure by it his love and devotion for his own people at Ars. Up to the time of the pilgrimages when he became the confessor of the world at large, he was accustomed frequently to visit his people in their own homes, and this was

G

done in his own kind and gentle way. Every day he set out about noon to call upon one or other of his sixty families, for of such the village was constituted. He could not, in the first days of his ministry, immediately begin to speak of religion, but confined his conversation to ordinary topics, such as the health of the family, their work, and their success or difficulties, but before leaving he would say some beautiful spiritual thing. His later visits, when he got to know his people well, were delightfully informal. He would enter whilst the family were seated at their midday meal, and he would remain standing, leaning against the wall, or a dresser or table; and although he still showed himself solicitous about their temporal concerns he soon got on to religious topics, and administered encouragement or blame as it appeared necessary. Rarely would he accept of any food, but if on occasions he did so this was never more than the smallest portion, such as a potato, or a little wine with water.

This personal visiting came to an end when his increased confession work rendered it impossible; and the task was entrusted to his assistant priest. But he never would surrender the privilege of visiting the sick, and would readily rise in the middle of the night, or early morning, to go to a stricken parishioner; and in the day time would leave his confessional for the same purpose. Even in the days of the thronged pilgrimages he would give hours to his own flock, whilst making visitors wait whole days for a few minutes' interview. Moreover he always gave his own people the earliest opportunities of coming to confession—visitors had to wait.

In the midst of this fruitful harvest of souls the saint never ceased to long for some years of solitude, for the twofold reason of relieving Ars of an indifferent and even unworthy pastor, for so in his deep humility he always considered himself, and of doing penance for his sins before he should be called to the judgment-seat of God. Time and again, therefore, he sought to be released from his post, and not until the last few years remaining to him did he surrender this desire. In the last decade of his life he conceived the idea of joining the Capuchins, but his friend Father Leonard of that Order, who occasionally acted as his confessor, dissuaded him and suggested instead his being enrolled as a Franciscan tertiary, and to this the Curé finally agreed.

Much earlier in his ministry at Ars, namely, in 1823, St. John Mary had hoped, as he afterwards confessed, to be suspended from office by the bishop and condemned to years of penance. The circumstances were as follows. After a long struggle he had succeeded in banishing open evil from his parish, and certain enemies in revenge accused him of shameful crimes, and even wrote letters to the new bishop of Belley, Mgr. Devie, containing scurrilous charges. The bishop who, so far, had not made the acquaintance of the saint, thought it advisable to send the parish priest of Trévoux to make investigations but when that priest sent in his report, the bishop was convinced not merely of the Curé's innocence, but also of his high sanctity. Nevertheless the saint felt keenly the attack on his priestly honour, and had even considered the advisability of resigning. But all through this bitter trial, although he knew the names of his detractors, he neither blamed nor even mentioned them by name. Heroic charity indeed!

But if he suffered joyfully trials and insults, he could not find it in his heart to rejoice when honours came his way, and when in 1852 the new bishop, Mgr. Chalandon, placed upon his shoulders, almost by force, the mozetta of an honorary canon, it is true to say that it caused him more pain than the terrible instruments of torture he wore constantly on his back. Very amusing it seemed to the Curé's friends to see him wriggling under his burden of honour, and looking "as though he had thorns on his back", but the last laugh was with the saint who sold the abhorred adornment for fifty francs, and gave the proceeds to the poor.

As all attempts to leave Ars were frustrated, St. John Mary, as he had feared, *died a parish priest*. But the fear he had felt all his life departed at the end, which was one of joy unalloyed. His death was one of the most joyful in all the annals of hagiography. The parish priest of Jassans, M. Beau, who for twenty years had been his ordinary confessor, and was constantly at his side during the last three days of his life, remarked that the fear of death which the Curé had before so frequently and so strongly manifested had completely vanished, "nor was the devil permitted to torment him in this supreme hour". The dying saint now realised to the full his own oft-quoted words, "How sweet it is to die if one has lived on the cross".

He died on the morning of August 4, 1859, the feast day of St. Dominic, one of God's greatest priests, and one whom he had in life much resembled, chiefly in those crowning virtues of a priest, penance and zeal for souls.

In 1904 Saint Pius X, himself a renowned parish priest, declared the Curé d'Ars Blessed, and in 1925 Pope Pius XI enrolled him in the calendar of the Saints. The same Pontiff four years later constituted him principal patron of the parochial clergy throughout the world.

For references to authorities for his life see Introduction.

39. BLESSED ANTHONY MARY PUCCI, O.S.M.,

"The Little Parish Priest."
Parish Priest of Viareggio. (1819-1892.)

IN the last of our short biographies of saintly parish priests we find a striking parallel with the life of St. Peter Fourier where sanctity was sought and found by a professed religious in the active work of a parish priest, sanctity declared heroic by the solemn authorization of the Church.

Blessed Anthony Mary Pucci was born on April 16, 1819, and baptised with the name of Eustace. His parents Anthony Pucci and Mary Oliva, née Macchi, were of peasant stock and lived at Poggiole in Tuscany where like nearly all their neighbours they remained true to their faith despite the anti-clerical influence then so rampant in the Italian

peninsula. Thus their son grew up in a completely
Catholic atmosphere. Signor Pucci who worked his
own little farm was also lay sacristan and his little
boy was in and out of the presbytery many times in
the week, and in fact received most of his education
there. As he grew older he helped in the work of
the farm, but after one particular visit to the shrine
of Our Blessed Lady at Boccadiro he felt he was
being drawn to serve God as a religious, and at the
age of eighteen was admitted to the novitiate of the
Servites at Florence where he received the habit in
December 1837 taking the name of Anthony Mary.
His ordination to the priesthood took place on
September 24, 1843, and in August of the next year
he was assigned to Viareggio near Pisa where the
Servites worked the parish of St. Andrew's, and
there he was made assistant to the parish priest, and
there he remained to the end of his long life, busied
all the time in parochial duties. To his parishioners
he was almost immediately known as "Il curatino",
the little parish priest, a title given to him rather
prematurely as he was only curate in our English use
of the word until the summer of 1847, when on July
26 he succeeded to the post of parish priest, although
only twenty-eight years of age. This charge he held
until his death forty-five years later.

Father Anthony was a man with few physical
gifts. Not only was he diminutive in stature, hence
the "curatino", but his countenance was rugged
rather than handsome. He was hesitant in conversation, had few of what men call the social graces
being almost excessively shy, and was never at home
with the "better class" of the parishioners "to whom

he went merely as a mendicant rather than a social equal''. Even in the pulpit he had none of the talents of an orator and had to learn his sermons by heart. His voice too was unattractive and nasal. And yet this was the man who together with Saint Pius X his contemporary shed more lustre on the office of parish priest than perhaps any other since the death of the Curé d'Ars. The secret of his success was his fixed determination to do his plain duty as a parish priest as long as he was entrusted with the office and to accomplish it with all the grace God gave him.

A large section of the population of Viareggio earned its living in the fishing trade or other occupations allied to it and consisted for the most part of practising Catholics, whereas the official class who depended for their living on the anticlerical government of Tuscany were willing slaves to the new freedom of thought and both hated and hindered the work of the Church. This anticlericalism hardened as the idea of a united Italy gradually took shape in the engulfing of the other kingdoms and independent states of the peninsula by the kingdom of Sardinia, and was finally accomplished in 1870 by the seizure of the States of the Church.

Amidst the turmoil of conflicting opinions and the violence that accompanied it Blessed Anthony went calmly on with his pastoral work, venerated by his parishioners and even respected by the civil administration. A marked feature of his pastorate was his careful visitation of his flock, a duty perhaps more neglected then than today. He made it a daily duty and always preceded it by a visit to the Blessed

Sacrament to bring a blessing on himself and those he was going to see, and to obtain the grace of showing himself not only a kind but a model priest. His complete absence of worldliness in these ministrations not unnaturally led his people to regard him with a respect not unmixed with awe, but he was far from seeming cold and distant and though he never came to a family on a mere friendly visit or as a material benefactor he was often the welcome bearer of much needed alms. He rapidly became the most respected and revered figure in Viareggio, and of far greater influence than any of its civil rulers without himself seeming to realise it.

But it was in the church where his principal work was done, teaching and administering the sacraments and above all offering the Holy Sacrifice. His devotion at Mass was the wonder of his people who beheld him day after day completely absorbed in the sacred mysteries and oblivious to all external happenings, once not even noticing an earth tremor that shook the building. One day a laybrother who was serving his Mass was startled to notice a space between Anthony's feet and the floor, and it was some moments before he was able to realize that the saint was slightly lifted up in the air. He naturally reported the matter to one of the fathers who however bade him keep the affair secret but asked him to let him know if the miracle occurred again. And it did. Several times.

Anthony was the perfect confessor. Kind but strict and uncompromising he spoke firmly but not bluntly; in fact it was generally noticed that in the confessional he possessed a fluency of speech which

consistently eluded him in the pulpit. In dealing
with distressed souls he was positively eloquent and
always so completely the loving shepherd that none
could take offence at any of his corrections.   His
confessional was besieged for hours each day, and
he would be seated there daily from four in the
morning until his Mass and after his thanksgiving he
would return until midday.   And there was always
a long evening session. He was always ready to hear
those who were shy of being seen coming to
confession and who crept to the church like
Nicodemus under cover of night.   These he would
gladly hear at any hour. With the dying he would
watch if possible right up to the end, even if it meant,
as it often did, staying up all night. When accused
of imprudently shortening his life by these practices
he would remind his critics that it is not necessary
to live a long life, but that it is a duty to make the
most of our opportunities.

As we have already said, amidst the great move-
ments of history in Italy he appeared to pass his
life in the tranquil existence of parish duties, but
this would not have pleased the devil, and therefore
it is not surprising to read that he too suffered
contradiction.   There were hardened sinners to
contend with, and also the irreligious societies every-
where springing up vowed to destroy the Church
and the civilization for which she stood. Her enemies
were his, and on one occasion one of them, a man
to whom he had shown many kindnesses, on the plea
of a sick call entrapped him in a lonely part of the
town and cruelly beat him.   Discovered in a badly
wounded condition Anthony was carried back to

the priory but refused to reveal the traitor's name. This was not a solitary case, but the saint bore all such trials cheerfully and continued to bring peace and comfort to all who would receive him.

In 1854 and 1855 the cholera appeared in Viareggio and through all that dreadful time Anthony slept near the front door, ready at a moment to be called to the dying. In caring for the sick he was heroically helped by a group of devoted women under Catherine Lenci, and when the scourge had passed the municipality could not forbear expressing their admiration and wished to give public recognition to Anthony and Catherine, but neither would accept it. Catherine and her companions were later formed into the congregation of Servite Mantellate nuns and she became Sister Juliana, O.S.M.

We may be allowed to wonder why Anthony was left so long in Viareggio. It is strange that a friar who had done so much should not have been called upôn to exercise his undoubted influence and gifts in a higher post. At any rate there he was and there he was to remain until his death, but in 1883 when he had already spent thirty-eight years in Viareggio his brethren seem to have woken up to the fact that they themselves were missing something of his wonderful fatherly care and accordingly elected him Provincial of the Tuscan Province but even this appointment did not sever him from his parochial duties and he retained the parish in addition to his work as chief superior. That he was in no way lacking in his duties as Provincial through doing double duty was proved by his re-election to that office in 1886.

He finally laid down the Provincialship in 1889 but remained on as parish priest working as usual until six days before his death. On the feast of the Epiphany, 1892, he sang High Mass but was so weak and trembling at the end of it that he had to take to his bed, where he died tranquilly and holily on January 12. The sorrow throughout the town was great and even genuine sympathy was expressed from the town hall where the municipality decreed a day of public mourning for his burial. Sixty years later, on June 22, 1952, Pius XII solemnly beatified this great Servite priest in St. Peter's, a priest who whilst living as a model religious under rule also lived nearly all his long life as a model parish priest.

Acta Apostolicae Sedis, July 1, 1952, pp. 488, 489; The Little Parish Priest—Blessed Anthony Pucci, C.T.S., 1952.

Index

PAGE